J. K. ROWLING

The Wizard Behind
Harry Potter

MARC SHAPIRO

ST. MARTIN'S GRIFFIN
NEW YORK

This Book Is Dedicated to

All the good people. My wife, Nancy. My daughter, Rachael. My mother, Selma. My agent, Lori. Bennie and Freda. Keri, Bad Baby, Chaos. Mike Kirby, Steve Ross. And finally to J. K. Rowling for lighting up the imagination of a whole generation. All good thoughts to you.

www.stmartins.com

Design by Nancy Resnick

ISBN-13: 978-0-312-37697-0
ISBN-10: 0-312-37697-9

Revised and Updated Edition: May 2007

10   9   8   7   6   5   4   3   2   1

SOURCES

Since Harry Potter burst on the scene, J. K. Rowling has been the subject of many press articles and has given many interviews. I found the following publications, with their high level of professionalism, particularly helpful: the Associated Press, *The Australian*, *Book*, *The Boston Globe*, *CBBC Newsround*, *Current Biography*, *Daily Mirror*, *Daily Telegraph* (London), the *Edinburgh Evening News*, *Entertainment Weekly*, *Good Housekeeping*, *The Guardian* (London), *The High*, *The Hollywood Reporter*, the *Los Angeles Times*, *Maclean's*, *The New*

SOURCES

York Times, Newsweek, The Observer (London), *People, Reader's Digest, School Library Journal, The Scotsman,* the *Sun, Sunday Herald,* The *Sunday Mirror, The Sunday Telegraph, Time, Time* (Europe), *The Times* (London), *Toronto Star, Variety,* and *The Washington Post.*

The following Web sites also helped in this journey: J. K. Rowling: Raincoast Kids; Meet J. K. Rowling: Scholastic.com; J. K. Rowling: Bookwire; The Unofficial Harry Potter Fan Club Page; Harry Potter: Scholastic.com; The Essential Harry Potter; books: BBC Online as well as Barnes and Noble.com; CNN.com; The Leaky Cauldron; ICulture; Salon.com; Empireonline; Upcoming Movies.com; Bloomsbury Magazine.com; and CBC.com.

Readers should be aware that Internet Web sites listed in this work may have changed or disappeared between when this work was written and when it is read.

CONTENTS

CONTENTS

I LOVE TO READ

I confess, I love to read.

After a hard day's work, there is no better way to wind down and relax than by curling up in a soft, comfortable chair, putting my feet up on an equally soft stool, and flipping through the pages of a good book as my cat, Chaos, purrs contentedly in my lap. What I read depends on what kind of mood I'm in.

Sometimes I want to find out about real people and real lives, so I will pick up a biography. But there are also those times when reading about the real world is the last thing on my mind. That is when I will pick up a science fiction story, a spooky thriller, or a Harry Potter book . . .

And escape to a place I've never been before.

There has always been a sense of comfort in escaping into a world of fantasy. Which is why the adventures of Harry Potter are so much fun for children and adults alike. There are, quite simply, no rules in a Harry Potter book—or at least none that cannot be broken in the name of fun and adventure.

We can have adventures in the land of Muggle that we cannot have anywhere else. As we flip through the pages of *Harry Potter and the Sorcerer's Stone* or *Harry Potter and the Chamber of Secrets*, we can close our eyes and pretend we've just finished a rousing game of Quidditch and are now back in the hallowed halls of Hogwarts, learning the fine arts of charms, spells, and magic, alongside good friends Ron and Hermione, at the feet of Professor Dumbledore.

Entering the world of Harry Potter is like following Alice down the rabbit hole into Wonderland. It is a place where just about anything can happen and usually does. Some of what goes on is truly frightening. I would not want to meet Voldemort or the Dementor on a dark night. But I sure would love to rip open a Howler and have it scream out its message to me. Traveling by way of Floo Powder would sure beat being stuck in rush-hour traffic. And I doubt anyone could find a better friend than Ron or Hermione.

The sign of a good fantasy is that the reader can lose himself or herself in it. And it goes without saying that millions of children and adults around the world have done just that with the adventures of Harry Potter.

But being curious, we also have questions. How did the author come up with those ideas? What does the person who created Harry look like? What color is her hair? After we have enjoyed our trip to fantasyland, we eventually want to know all about her.

What is the person like who writes Harry Potter stories?

Is she young or old? Happy or sad? Does she live alone, or does she write these fantastic stories with a brood of children underfoot? Did she have a happy childhood or was her family life so unhappy she was driven to escape into the world of fantasy?

Those were the questions I wanted to have answered. Which is why I set out to write *J. K. Rowling: The Wizard Behind Harry Potter.*

Often the story behind the author is as interesting, if not more so, than what is written. In the case of J. K. Rowling, the story has a little bit of everything. There is happiness and love. There is also some sadness. The story of J. K. Rowling is also one of bravery, determination, and triumph over seemingly overwhelming odds.

And finally there is the happy ending. The life of J. K. Rowling sounds very much like the stories she writes and is, in a way, a fairy tale come to life.

Knowing about J. K. Rowling and how she came to write the most popular books in the whole wide world will not change your feelings about Harry Potter. But *J. K. Rowling: The Wizard Behind Harry Potter* will definitely give you the story behind the story.

And knowing more will only add to the enjoyment the next time you sit in your chair or crawl into bed and pull the covers up tight . . .

And disappear into the land of Harry Potter one more time.

INTRODUCTION

I am back to my comfortable chair and my good book.

Chaos is purring.

It is time to turn the page.

—Marc Shapiro

1

WILD ABOUT HARRY

Sometimes the real world can be a confusing place. It is not always fair or kind. And in the real world there are not always happy endings. Which is why, every once in a while, we like to escape into the world of fantasy—a place where things always go our way and there is always a happy ending.

We want to believe in fantastic creatures in imaginary lands. We want to believe in magic powers, good friends, and the power of good to triumph over evil. We all fantasize about being able to fly and lift buildings off the ground. And how good a magic sword would feel in our hand as we go off to slay a dragon or win the hand of a beautiful princess.

Which is why we like Superman, Peter Pan, Mary Poppins, and the amazing adventures of Frodo in *The Lord of the Rings*. And it is why we are all now Potterites who can't wait for the further adventures of our favorite wizard, Harry Potter, a thirteen-year-old English orphan who attends the Hogwarts School of Witchcraft and Wizardry and tries to be a normal boy while confronting the truly fantastic at every turn.

The author of the Harry Potter books, J. K. (Joanne Kathleen) Rowling, is a grown woman with a child of her own. She is sensible, modest, and realistic—all good qualities when it comes to being a good parent and a positive member of the real world. She likes to walk the streets of her hometown of Edinburgh, Scotland. She will sit for hours at her favorite café, sipping an espresso and watching as the world passes her by.

But there is something that sets J. K. Rowling apart from the rest of us. For Joanne Kathleen Rowling likes to dream at all hours of the day and night. She dreams of faraway lands, bigger-than-life good guys, truly evil bad guys, and likable young children who try and make sense of it all. But unlike others, she turns her dreams into reality when she sits down with pen and paper and begins to write about the adventures of Harry Potter.

A smile crosses her face. Her already expressive eyes, framed by long wavy hair, grow even wider. Her pen slashes across the paper like a lightning bolt. In her mind, a door to a delightful new world of imagination and wonder has just opened wide and she is about to pass through it.

When J. K. Rowling sits down to give new life to Harry Potter, usually in her favorite writing place, a café called Nicholson's, a change comes over the author. Because to create the latest adventure of Harry, his good friends Ron Weasley and Hermione Granger, and their adventures, Joanne has to stop being an adult and become a child who also wants to believe in the unbelievable.

And once Joanne becomes that child, almost anything can and does happen.

From the opening passages of *Harry Potter and the Sorcerer's Stone*, we can sense that something quite out of the ordinary is up. Our introduction to Harry is not a happy one. He is an orphan who has been living for ten years in a closet under the stairs of his cruel aunt and uncle's house. But we soon discover that Harry is not an ordinary soul. He is the son of wizards. However, Harry does not have a clue that he even has these powers until one day a giant appears out of nowhere and delivers to Harry a scholarship to the Hogwarts School of Witchcraft and Wizardry.

Once there, Harry discovers friends, foes, his magical powers, and a mission to get rid of the evil that lies hidden in the depths of the school. In the classic sense, friends unite, evil is banished, at least temporarily, and all is well.

There is much more of the same in *Harry Potter and the Chamber of Secrets,* as a more mature Harry and his friends once again battle evil while the young wizard begins to learn more about his adopted land. And what he finds, thanks to Joanne's vivid imagination, is surprises around every corner. There is the diary that writes back, a dead professor who continues to teach class, and portraits of long-dead ancestors who come alive at night to primp and curl their hair.

By the third book, *Harry Potter and the Pris-*

oners of Azkaban, the author has seen fit to darken things up. In the Dementors, we see truly disgusting evil. But Harry has by this time grown wise enough and powerful enough to fight the good fight. There is also that priceless moment when Harry discovers Cho Chan on the Quidditch field and thinks to himself that she is kind of pretty.

Joanne has filled the page with enticing images and has us hooked.

"I really can, with no difficulty at all, think myself back to eleven years old," said Rowling in a *Time* magazine interview of her ability to tap into her own childhood when writing. "I can remember being a kid and being very powerless and having this whole underworld that to adults is always going to be impenetrable. I think that I have very vivid memories of how it felt to be Harry's age."

On more than one occasion, Joanne has acknowledged her childhood memories as an influence. For her, Hermione is very much herself as a child. And while there was no real-life Harry in her life, she has said that many elements of the character have come from people she knew. And her enemies? They spring to life when Joanne remembers the times when she had to face the school bully and did not know whether she would come out okay.

The author has said that what she likes about writing the adventures of Harry Potter, and what brings her willingly to the task every day, is the notion of opening up a world of dreams and its possibilities.

"When you dream, you can do what you like," she has told *Newsweek*.

And there have been dreams aplenty in the first three Harry Potter adventures, *Harry Potter and the Philosopher's Stone* (retitled *Harry Potter and the Sorcerer's Stone* in America), *Harry Potter and the Chamber of Secrets*, and *Harry Potter and the Prisoner of Azkaban*. The world Harry Potter inhabits is dotted with strange creatures like Buckbeak, Scabbers, and Crookshanks. There are good people like Professor Dumbledore and Hagrid and bad people like the Dursleys and the evil Lord Voldemort. In the world of Harry Potter, owls run banks, apprentice students chase after balls on flying broomsticks, and apprentice wizards tread lightly as they enter the Forbidden Forest.

But finally it is Harry Potter, a skinny thirteen-year-old with glasses, green eyes, and a head of unruly black hair who is the heart and soul of J. K. Rowling's adventures. The author feels that Harry is a mirror into her young readers' souls.

"Harry is smart and good at sports and a lot of things that other children would like to be," Rowling once told an interviewer. "But children also feel for him because he has lost his parents. If an author makes a character an orphan, few children will want to be an orphan too. But it is a freeing thing because a certain weight of parental expectation is lifted."

Yet the adventures of Harry Potter are much more than merely escape for the preteen set. Adults have also taken Harry to their hearts and marvel at the simplicity and positive values presented in the tales. Harry often is the center of a family's time together. Parents read to their children and children often read out loud to their parents. Or parents, after their children have gone to sleep, have been known to sit down with the book and read it themselves.

The author regularly reads her fan mail and so is well aware that the power of Harry Potter to capture readers has spanned the generations. A woman from Glasgow, Scotland, recently wrote to

Joanne's British publisher asking how to go about joining the Harry Potter Fan Club, adding as an aside that she was sixty years old. An Englishman, when inquiring about the possibility of a Harry Potter movie, described himself as "a child at heart, an adult in body." She has had reports of family squabbles breaking out at bedtime when a parent wanted to finish reading a chapter and ended up taking the book from her children so she could read the book herself.

Joanne has thought long and hard about why people of all ages respond to Harry, and she thinks she knows the reason why.

"I think some of the reason is that Harry has to accept adult burdens in his life, although he is a child," she said in a recent interview. "There's something very endearing about that to kids and adults as well. Harry is also an old-fashioned hero. There's enough human frailty in Harry that people of all ages can identify with."

The author also points to a sense of morality that runs through each book. Rather than preach, she gets her messages across quite naturally and humanly in the actions and thoughts of her characters. As we have discovered in the first four books,

Harry Potter is not the perfect little boy. He bends and breaks the rules when it suits his purpose and has all the insecurities of a normal boy or girl. Children and adults tend to love the fact that they can open a Harry Potter book and see themselves in the characters.

Arthur Levine, the U.S. editor of the Harry Potter books, feels that a big attraction to readers is the idea of growing up underappreciated, feeling like an outcast, and then suddenly bursting forth into the light and being discovered. "That is the fantasy of every person who grows up smart but not very athletic. That's the emotional connection that drew me to the books," he told *The New York Times.*

Whatever the reason, Harry Potter has become a worldwide phenomenon since the publication of the first book in 1997. To date, the first four books have sold more than 10 million copies in over a hundred different languages. The books continue to reside at or near the top of a number of best-seller lists, and a movie studio is in the process of making a big-budget movie of *Harry Potter and the Sorcerer's Stone* that will be in movie theaters all over when this edition of the book is out!

But there is more to the popularity of Harry Potter than book sales and movie deals. Kids have taken Harry to their hearts, and he has become a very real part of their playtime. They have made up games and put on plays centered around Harry and his adventures. Many of the numerous computer Web sites that have sprung up around the Harry Potter books feature original stories written by fans. Groups of children gather regularly to read Harry Potter out loud. One enterprising eleven-year-old even had "Educated at Hogwarts" printed up on business cards so he could hand them out to his friends.

Surprisingly, the author behind the fantastic adventures of Harry Potter is a person of relatively simple pleasures and tastes. She told an Internet site that she has no hobbies "except hanging out with my friends and writing." Her favorite holiday is Halloween. Her favorite television shows are British comedies and the U.S. imports *Frasier* and *The Simpsons.*

"I get bored with my life," she once said. "I prefer inventing things."

But for Rowling, the true joy comes in the stories of how young children have embraced her tales. And they certainly have. A family in California was so anxious to read *Harry Potter and the Prisoner of Azkaban* that they went on the Internet and ordered a British copy of the book so that they would not have to wait months for the book to be published in America. When her third book went on sale at 3:45 P.M., the precise moment when English schools let out for the day, she was amazed when stores sold out every copy in a matter of minutes.

Rowling, who is often shy about doing interviews and has proven very secretive when asked about the further adventures of Harry, came to enjoy book tours. In fact, she gets a lot of pleasure from book signings, when she gets to meet her young audience face-to-face. One example of this occurred during a visit to a school in England when she was approached by a young boy carrying one of her books. "He recited the first page of the first book to me from memory," she explained to *Newsweek*. "When he stopped, he said, 'I can go on.' He continued reciting the first five pages of the book. That was unbelievable."

However, she said, during a *Scholastic* online chat, one of her most gratifying moments came about during a reading and book signing appearance in her hometown of Edinburgh. "The event was sold out and the queue for signing at the end was very long. When a twelve-year-old girl finally reached me, she said, 'I didn't want there to be so many people here, because this is my book!' I told her that was exactly how I feel about my favorite books. Nobody else has a right to know them, let alone like them!"

What can best be described as Pottermania occurred last year when Joanne came to the United States on yet another book tour. Her many stops at bookstores across the country continued to amaze her and showed the author that while Harry Potter books are written in a distinctly British style, the messages of her books are international.

During a reading in a high school gymnasium in Santa Rosa, California, Joanne was shocked when she looked out and saw 2,500 Harry Potter fans jumping up and down on the bleachers and shouting "Harry! Harry!" at the top of their lungs.

The scene repeated itself in San Francisco, California, when Joanne's car rounded a corner and the writer was amazed to find more than a thousand people standing in line in front of a bookstore for a 9:30 A.M. reading and autograph session. She would later discover that many of the children and their parents had spent the night in line just so they could make sure they would get in for the event. One family had even made the six-hour trip by car from Los Angeles the night before just so they could be first in line. Joanne gave a short reading, answered her fan's many questions, and then signed a thousand books in two hours. And then, quick as a flash, she was back inside her limo and gone.

"It was a little like having the Beatles here," said an excited, out-of-breath bookstore representative to *Entertainment Weekly* after the event. "Kids will probably be coming here for years saying 'Wow! That's where the Harry Potter lady was standing.' "

For J. K. Rowling, the success of Harry Potter has been a fantasy all its own. After years of struggles in unfulfilling jobs, living in poverty, and trying to make a go of it as a single mother, the author now lives comfortably in Scotland and regularly travels around the world. She has often reflected on how her reaction to the success of Harry "has been shock" and that "it was like being catapulted into fairyland."

"I always find it difficult to be objective about Harry," she once admitted to BBC Online when discussing the question of reality and fantasy in her books. "To me, they remain my own private little world. For five years, they were my own private secret. From the moment I had the idea for the book, I could see a lot of comic potential in the idea that wizards walk among us."

But finally J. K. Rowling's success is a dream come true. "I would have been crazy to have expected what has happened to Harry," she has said. "The mere fact of being able to say I was a published author was the fulfillment of a dream I've had since I was a very young child."

2

RABBIT AND MISS BEE

J. K. Rowling's parents met on a train in 1963. And as in all good fairy tales, it was love at first sight.

At first look Peter Rowling and his bride-to-be could not have been more different. Peter was the manager of an aircraft factory, while Ann worked as a lab technician. He came from a blue-collar world, while she was into books and more intellectual pursuits. However, none of those differences seemed to matter.

Because as they courted, fell in love, and eventually decided to get married, they discovered that they did indeed have a lot in common. They shared a good sense of humor, and both believed in the importance of home and family life. They also loved the English countryside and good books. When they walked down the aisle, Peter and Ann felt that they had each found the perfect mate.

Shortly after their marriage, Peter and Ann moved into a small but comfortable home in the tiny hamlet of Chipping Sodbury. The couple loved the idea of living literally in the middle of England's famed forests and hillsides. But they had always been city dwellers, so they enjoyed their regular trips into the nearby town of Bristol, where they would shop and idle away the hours together.

Peter and Ann felt they had the perfect life. Only one thing could enrich their story.

And that came in November 1965, when the couple announced to family and friends that Ann was pregnant with their first child. The next nine months were a joyous and exciting time for Peter and Ann as they made preparations for the arrival of their child. They speculated about whether their child would be a boy or a girl and discussed names for the child at great length. They regularly wandered into the room that had been picked out as the baby's room and planned where the crib would be and what colors the walls should be painted.

As is true of all parents, they hoped that the child would be healthy and happy. Late in July 1966, Peter's car pulled up in front of Chipping Sodbury General Hospital. It was time.

Joanne Kathleen Rowling came kicking and screaming into the world on July 31, 1966. In later years, Joanne would look back on the occasion of her birth as an omen of things to come. "I think it is rather appropriate for someone who collects funny names to be born in a hospital named Chipping Sodbury," she laughed in an online biography.

Almost from the moment Joanne was born, Peter and Ann sensed the bright, inquisitive nature of their child. Her eyes were always wide in amazement at the world around her, and she was always grasping and touching things with curiosity. They could almost predict that one of the first words out of their daughter's mouth would be *why*.

Joanne once described her early childhood years as "dreamy." The young child seemed to have a knack for solitary pursuits. She often played imaginary games in her room or in the tall grass in her backyard. If there was a tree around, she would climb it. If other children approached her, Joanne was quick to invite them to join her in any number of games. Even in those early years, she was very fond of the idea of "let's pretend."

Hoping to nurture their child's imagination, Joanne's parents began reading to her at an early age. Because both parents were constant readers, it is no surprise that one of the author's earliest memories was of "the house being full of books and of my parents constantly reading to me." Joanne was fed a steady diet of fairy tales and fantasy books as well as a smattering of the classics.

Even during her most uncomfortable moments, the sounds of her parents reading to her always had a calming effect.

"My most vivid memory of childhood is my father sitting and reading *The Wind in the Willows* to me," she told the London *Daily Telegraph*. "I had the measles at the time, but I don't really remember that. I just remember the book."

What her parents did not realize was that a constant exposure to literature—in particular, to fairy tales and stories of the fantastic—had made an enormous impression on the young child. She began to dream up fantastic, well-plotted stories with larger-than-life characters. When she was at play, her stories were full of character and detail light-years beyond those generally produced by a child of her age.

Although she was too young to think in terms of what she wanted to be when she grew up, Joanne Kathleen Rowling, at a very early age, had this image of herself as somebody who would put pencil to paper and create magic worlds. "Writing for me has always been a kind of wonderful compulsion," she said in a 1999 interview of her early inclination to write. "I don't think anyone could have made me do it or could have prevented me from doing it. It's weird, but writing is all I ever wanted to do."

But these were private thoughts for Joanne, that wonderful secret that kept her warm and cozy in her bed at night and helped her to glide through her days. To tell even her parents would have ended all the fun.

But when her younger sister, Di, born less than two years after Joanne, reached age three, five-year-old Joanne "was big enough to hold her" sister down, so she began making up tall tales about fantastic creatures and imaginary places and telling them to Di.

These stories would often center on rabbits because, as Joanne has recalled, "we badly wanted a rabbit." One of the most memorable of these early flights of fantasy, and the one that always had Di roaring with little-girl laughter and excitement, was a story about how Di had fallen down a rabbit hole one day and ended up being fed strawberries by the rabbit family.

More often than not Di would sit fascinated by her older sister's tales. She would inevitably ask Joanne to tell her the same story again and again, and because the stories were not written down, they would often come out slightly different in the retelling. Joanne was encouraged by her younger sister's response to begin jotting her stories down on paper. So one day, not long after she turned six, Joanne sat down with pencil and paper and wrote her first story.

Not surprisingly, it was a story about a rabbit called Rabbit. Out of this child came a fanciful tale of a rabbit who got the measles and was visited by a number of friends, including a giant bee named Miss Bee. "I wrote stories about rabbits for a couple of years. I definitely had a rabbit fixation," she once told an interviewer.

Di was thrilled with the story. Joanne's parents, who had taken to eavesdropping on their daughter's fantasy games, were amused by their daughter's imagination but did not feel it necessary to encourage her in any way. But their encouragement was not really necessary, because Joanne had already made up her mind that she was going to be a writer. "Ever since Rabbit and Miss Bee, I knew I wanted to be a writer," she told *School Library Journal.* "I cannot overstate how much I wanted that. But I would rarely tell anyone so. I just never really spoke about it because I was embarrassed. And because my parents were the kind of parents who would have thought 'Ah yes, that's very nice, dear. But where is the pension plan?' "

Joanne grew into a bright child whose imagination was often the talk of the neighborhood. This talent was also a topic during her first years in school, when her teachers would marvel at the maturity and creativity of her early reports and papers. Joanne took these early compliments as a sign that she had found something she was good at.

Another one of the young girl's early attempts

at storytelling was a story of chills and adventure called *The Seven Cursed Diamonds.* "At that age I thought it was a novel," she would recall in later years. "But I think now that it was only a very long short story."

Joanne was doing more than writing during those early years. It was the rare moment when her parents did not find her nose buried in a book. The young child was quite outgoing and had a number of friends in the neighborhood but always seemed to prefer to go off by herself and read. Among her favorites was *The Little White Horse* by Elizabeth Goudge, *Manxmouse* by Paul Gallico, and the Narnia books by C. S. Lewis.

"I adored E. Nesbit," she once said of her reading habits. "I think her books are wonderful. I also liked Noel Streatfeild, who did those girly books about ballet shoes and things. Even now, if I was in a room with one of the Narnia books, I would pick it up and re-read it like a shot," she explained to the London *Telegraph.*

Shortly after Joanne began to write, her parents decided that they needed a bigger home and moved the family to the small town of Yate, just outside of Bristol. Less than a year after they moved to Yate, Peter and Ann decided that they liked the scenery better on the other side of Bristol and moved the family to yet another small town, Winterbourne.

Joanne and Di adjusted to the moves just fine and were quick to make friends with the neighborhood children. Winterbourne, in particular, had a lot of children Joanne and Di's age; they were immediately welcomed into the informal gang that would play games up and down the streets of the town. In those days, Joanne was very much a tomboy, engaging in just about every rough-and-tumble game without worrying about falling down and hurting herself. Even at that age, Joanne was not what you would call athletic and would often fall. But her persistence in trying soon gained her the respect of the neighborhood children.

Two of her closest friends in Winterbourne were a brother and sister named Ian and Vikki Potter. In later years, Ian Potter would tell *Book* magazine that when his sister and he would get together with Joanne and her sister, they would occasionally tell stories. "But most of all we liked dressing up, and nine times out of ten, it would be Joanne who would say, 'Oh, let's play witches and wizards.' "

Joanne remembered being quite close to Ian and Vikki during their days in Winterbourne. One reason for their friendship was their name.

"Their surname was Potter," she once recalled. "I always liked the name."

3

CHILDISH THINGS

Shortly after Joanne Kathleen Rowling turned nine, her parents decided it was time to move once again. Only this time it was because her parents' dream had finally come true.

Peter and Ann Rowling had both been born and raised in London and were basically city folk at heart. But because it was cheaper to live in the country, they had postponed any notion of living in a city. However, as Peter moved up in his job as a mechanic for an automobile factory and began receiving a higher salary, the couple decided it was time to make the move.

The couple, despite their yearning for city life, had grown to like the presence of forests and hillsides in their life. Rather than a big city, the Rowlings decided small would be better.

Tutshill is a small village situated near Chepstow in the Forest of Dean. It was very much a city with streets, stores, and schools. But the river Wye ran by and there were fields all around, making it the ideal mixture of city and country.

Joanne and Di quickly adjusted to their new surroundings. They would frolic for hours by the river and make up fantasy games to carry out in the fields. Joanne was outgoing and soon made friends in her neighborhood. When she felt comfortable enough, she would bring out some of her stories and read them to the neighborhood kids. While the other children did not quite know what to make of this little girl who used big words and told funny stories about fantastic places, they were impressed and gladly made room for a regular storytime from Joanne.

She would continue to enjoy playground activities, but reading and writing, which are solitary pursuits, remained first on her list of passions.

When it came to books, she was already reading well beyond her grade level. At age nine, Joanne discovered Ian Fleming's James Bond novels, and they became a regular part of her reading pastime.

Not too long after that she discovered the works of Jane Austen and was never the same again. Austen's delicate passages and detailed stories became a model for Joanne Rowling. "Jane Austen is my favorite author, ever."

There was only one drawback to living in the town of Tutshill. Joanne had to go to Tutshill Primary School. And Joanne hated her new school.

"It was a very small, very old-fashioned place," she painfully remembered for the Okubooks Web site. "The rolltop desks still had inkwells."

But that was not the only problem Joanne had with the school. There was her new teacher, Mrs. Morgan, to deal with. And Mrs. Morgan scared the life out of Joanne. Mrs. Morgan was a strict, no-nonsense type of teacher who taught her class according to the book. Unfortunately for Joanne,

Mrs. Morgan's book and her new student did not agree when it came to mathematics.

"She gave me an arithmetic test on the very first morning, and, after a huge effort, I managed to get zero right out of ten," she said on an Okubooks chat. "The test was on fractions and I had never done fractions before."

On her first day, Mrs. Morgan sat Joanne in a row of desks to the far right of the classroom. The young child was fine with that until a few days later when she figured out, by talking to her fellow students, that the teacher had put her in the stupid row.

It seemed that Mrs. Morgan had made up her seating chart based on how clever she thought her students were. The brightest students sat on the left side of the room and the rest sat on the right. Joanne painfully recalled her first days at Tutshill Primary, when, she wrote, "I was as far right as I could get without sitting on the playground."

It was a tough first year for Joanne. She was not making friends as easily as she had in the past. Physically and emotionally she was changing. It all added up to a rough beginning in her new school.

"I wasn't as clever as I thought I should be," she confessed when looking back on those days for

Salon magazine. "I don't think I was a know-it-all. I was obsessed with achieving academically, but that masked a huge insecurity. I think it is very common for plain young girls to feel this way. I definitely would not want to go back and do childhood again. I don't look back on it as a phase of blissful happiness at all."

She was the new kid in school, and she had to deal with the embarrassment of being identified as dumb. But Joanne managed to turn the experience around.

She studied hard and managed to make a small but loyal circle of friends. Not surprisingly, English was her best subject. Although she continued to write fantasy fables in her spare moments, she was not comfortable with sharing them with anybody but Di and one or two of her closest friends.

Joanne was determined to prove her teacher's impression of her wrong; by the end of the year, she had convinced Mrs. Morgan that she was not a dim bulb. One day she was rewarded when her teacher told her she could now sit on the left side of the classroom. Joanne recalled the promotion with mixed emotions.

"I had been promoted to second left. But the promotion was at a cost. Mrs. Morgan made me swap seats with my best friend. So in one short walk across the room, I became clever but unpopular," she said in her Web site entry.

Joanne regained her popularity and continued through her primary school years in an uneventful way. Her grades continued to be good. She remained painfully shy, with only a small circle of close friends. Writing continued to be her passion.

No matter how busy her days were, she always managed to find some quiet time to release her fantasies. Her stories, full of magic and funny characters with even funnier names, were the highlight of her sister's playtime. The praise Joanne received from Di and her parents convinced Joanne, even as young as she was, that she would one day be an important writer and would live a wonderful, fairy-tale life.

Joanne successfully graduated from Tutshill Primary and was soon on her way to Wyedean Comprehensive School for middle school. The confidence and positive self-image that Joanne had fought hard to cultivate during elementary school disappeared during her first year at Wyedean Comprehensive.

She became insecure at the prospect of attending school with older children. Plus she was going through puberty and thus felt very insecure. It also did not help that she wore glasses. "I was quiet, freckly, short-sighted, and rubbish at sports," she once said.

But Joanne managed to find her niche at Wyedean. Eventually she found other girls like her—quiet, smart, and not quite popular—and she became a part of that group. She did quite well in school, with English and foreign languages being her favorite subjects.

The youngster slowly began to come out of her shell at Wyedean. She was continuing to write and finally felt confident enough to risk it all by reading some of her stories to her new friends. They liked what they heard and were regularly entertained by Joanne's creative efforts.

"I used to tell my equally quiet and studious friends long serial stories during lunchtime," she wrote in an essay. "They usually involved us all doing heroic and daring deeds we certainly would not have done in real life."

Joanne breezed through her comprehensive school years on a steady course with relatively few noteworthy achievements. There was the embarrassment of breaking her arm one day while playing the very noncontact sport of net ball. There was also the day Joanne became the big girl on campus when she was attacked by the toughest girl in her grade. She would later recall that she would logically have preferred to run from trouble rather than stand and fight. But fight back is exactly what she ended up doing.

"I didn't have a choice," she once said. "It was hit back or lie down and play dead. For a few days I was quite famous because she hadn't managed to flatten me. The truth was, my locker was right behind me and it held me up."

Unfortunately, Joanne's newfound reputation as a tough girl lasted only a short time. She soon reverted to timidity and would spend weeks peering nervously around corners, in constant fear of being ambushed.

Through her later years in comprehensive school, Joanne began to come out of her shell. Her confidence growing, she was now quicker to speak up in class and was more assertive in nonschool conversations and activities. While still what would be considered very unathletic, she was now more inclined to mix it up with the other girls. This, she would later report, was due in part to the fact that her glasses had been replaced by contact lenses, so she was less fearful of getting hit in the face.

In fact, Joanne, by her own reports, flowered in her teen years. She felt that, personally and socially, things had actually begun to get better and she finally came to the all-important realization that there was more to Joanne Kathleen Rowling than someone who was driven to get everything right. Joanne was suddenly very comfortable with herself.

Like most normal teenagers, Joanne had a growing sense of independence; this would lead to the occasional row with her parents, usually short-lived arguments over very little. Her relationship with Di remained close. When not helping her younger sibling with her homework, Joanne would continue to use Di as her first audience for the many stories she was continuing to write. The second group to hear her latest tales was her girl-friends at school.

Despite the fact that she had numerous teachers who saw something in her and encouraged her in a creative direction, writing remained a largely private pursuit. The stories she felt confident enough to share were often the tales of action and adventure that featured herself and her friends as thinly disguised characters in stories of derring-do.

Her other stories, those she perceived as more intimate, she would not show to anyone. These were the stories that she felt a real writer would write. And she was not quite ready to let the outside world into that part of her creative life.

Joanne's love for reading continued to blossom as well. She had long since begun to read about the lives of real people and had developed a particular infatuation for author Jessica Mitford, a feminist who ran off and joined the Spanish Civil War at age nineteen and was a passionate supporter of human rights. "I remember reading the book *Hons and Rebels* at age fourteen, and it changed my life."

Joanne had grown into quite the confident student in her senior year at Wyedean Comprehensive. She was popular and outgoing, and her grades were quite good. So good, in fact, that Joanne was made Head Girl in her final year.

Head Girl was a lofty position that all the girls aspired to. But, in fact, very little responsibility was attached to the title. Once a year, when some noblewoman from the region came to visit the school, it was the job of the Head Girl to show her around the school fair. The requirement that Joanne dreaded the most was that the Head Girl also had to give a talk to the whole school.

"I decided to play them a record to cut down on the time that I had to speak to them," she laughingly recalled in a Web site memory. "Well, the record was scratched, and right in the middle of playing, it began skipping and played the same line over and over again. Finally the deputy headmistress came out on stage and kicked it."

Joanne ended her years at Wyedean Comprehensive with high honors. Her teachers were predicting a bright future for her. Her parents were proud. Joanne Kathleen Rowling was quiet on the subject of her future. She knew in her heart of hearts what she wanted to do with her life. She had her own hopes and dreams.

Now all she had to do was figure out how to make them come true.

4

LIFE LESSONS

Joanne wanted to write. But being admittedly "the most disorganized person in the whole world," she did not know how to begin. So she would write something, read through it, and usually find enough fault in her work to discard it. Even when she was happy with a story, it still remained her own private happiness.

She had boxes and folders full of short stories, but did not have a clue how one went about getting them published. She knew magazines bought such stories all the time but never saw fit to submit one. Plus, even thinking about doing so usually ended up with Joanne backing down in the face of her old fears of letting other people judge her work.

So, like so many others, Joanne was an eighteen-year-old with definite ideas but lacking the courage to carry them out. This was a side of herself that Joanne did not particularly like, and she would often upbraid herself for being too cowardly to extend herself. But the truth was that Joanne Kathleen Rowling was just not ready to take on the world.

Because Joanne was frustrated at her inability to take that next big step in her writing life, she was easily influenced by others. Consequently, she was willing to take her parent's advice.

Peter and Ann, having not been privy to her writing ambitions, had long been bewildered at their eldest daughter's seeming lack of direction. Joanne's parents had regularly suggested that with her love of language, their daughter should study French and literature, which would lead to a wonderful career as a bilingual legal secretary. And with her good grades, they felt Exeter University would be the ideal place for her to go.

Joanne's heart was in her writing and she felt

that pursuing any other line of work would be a mistake. However, being an obedient child, Joanne reluctantly took her parents' advice and was soon enrolled at Exeter.

The teenager was encouraged by the stories she had heard that Exeter was a liberal school that was big on unconventional ideas. She figured that, if nothing else, she would find much to influence her in her true passions. In fact, what she discovered shortly after enrolling was that Exeter was actually a conservative school wrapped up in traditional ideals. "It was fantastic," she told a reporter, "but it did not offer quite the chance to be a radical that I planned."

Joanne's years at Exeter were productive. She found that she was able to master French fairly easily. A big part of her education at Exeter was a year spent in Paris, learning to use the French language in a practical setting. Joanne found the year abroad exhilarating.

She took in the sights and marveled at being in another country for the first time without her family. Joanne grew up during that year in Paris. By the time she returned to Exeter, Joanne Kathleen

Rowling had grown confident in her ability to make her way in the world.

During this time Joanne had her first serious relationship. Being in love and having someone care about her was an important thing for her. Joanne reveled in the fact that she was, in fact, attractive enough and bright enough to gain the affections of a terrific boy.

Of course every spare moment was taken up with writing. There was the usual batch of short stories that only a handful of people ever saw. She also attempted a novel. But while she was confident in other areas, Joanne steadfastly refused to submit any of her stories, belittling them any time anyone would suggest that her stories were good and that she should send them out.

This lack of confidence in the thing she valued most haunted her every waking hour. In her heart, Joanne knew that it was time to shake off the bonds. Unfortunately her head still had a firm hold on her fears and insecurities. So she continued to do nothing at all.

Joanne graduated from Exeter with honors, and as often happens, she and her boyfriend naturally drifted apart. But Joanne had little time to grieve over a lost love. She was soon going out on her first job interviews.

Getting dressed up and presenting herself at job interviews was not something the young woman liked doing. It seemed like a silly, unnecessary game. It made her feel totally inadequate and very much like a little girl again. Besides, this was not what she really wanted to do, which was to write fabulous stories, see them published, and be able to keep writing, and live happily ever after. But since she was not willing to take the risks necessary to reach that pinnacle, Joanne would have to contend with the real world.

The next six years were a rough introduction to the often tedious life of the workaday world. Joanne went through a series of jobs. In one instance, she spent two years researching human rights violations for Amnesty International. While she felt she was doing important work and that her idol, Jessica Mitford, would approve, the work itself soon became predictable and boring, two things Joanne could not abide.

For the most part, she held a seemingly endless string of boring secretarial jobs. The work did not interest her and she was not making a lot of money. Plus, as she has readily admitted, "I later proved to be the worst secretary ever."

Her mind always seemed to be on something else. "Whatever job I had, I was always writing like crazy," she once wrote. "All I ever liked about offices was being able to type up stories on the computer when no one was looking. I was never paying much attention in meetings because I was usually scribbling bits of my latest stories in the margins of the pad or thinking up names for my characters. This is a problem when you're supposed to be taking the minutes of the meeting."

Needless to say, Joanne's employers frowned on her writing fantasy stories on company time, and she was dismissed from a couple of her jobs. But for the most part, Joanne simply got tired of doing work she detested and would eventually quit. Well into her twenties, the young woman was like a boat without a rudder.

Joanne's parents were supportive but concerned that their older daughter seemed to be having trouble finding her place in life. Her only solace in an otherwise bleak world was her writing.

"I was writing a lot of short stories and a lot of

started and abandoned novels," she told *School Library Journal* of that period in her life. "I felt I worked very hard and had served my apprenticeship in terms of writing." She felt less than positive about herself when those works would inevitably end up in a box with all the other stories that had not seen the light of day.

Unfortunately, all the hard work still did not add up to much, so Joanne reluctantly searched for yet another job. This time she found employment as an office worker for the Manchester Chamber of Commerce.

Joanne had another reason for going to Manchester. She had received a letter from her old boyfriend at Exeter, stating that he was in Manchester and that he'd like to see her again. The job she got was as dull and boring to her as all the others had been, but this time she was determined to make a go of things.

Joanne made time for her old boyfriend but remained diligent in her writing. At lunchtime, she would make her way to one of the nearby pubs or cafés, settle at an out-of-the-way table, and write. While far from antisocial, she would often find herself praying that nobody in the office was having a birthday or some other celebration that would require her to join in, taking up her precious writing time.

Joanne looked upon the commute between her London home and Manchester as her private time. She would often while away the time reading a book, working on her latest story, or simply staring out the window at the passing scenery. One day, as she returned to London after yet another day of unrewarding work, the train suddenly ground to a halt.

There was some kind of mechanical problem that, it was announced, would require a delay of about four hours. Normally this would have been ideal. But since Joanne was too tired to either read or write, she focused her attention on a group of cows, grazing in a meadow in front of her.

What she did not realize was that her life was about to change. "I was sitting on the train, just staring out the window at some cows. It was not the most inspiring subject. When all of a sudden the idea for Harry just appeared in my mind's eye. I can't tell you why or what triggered it. But I saw the idea of Harry and the wizard school very plainly. I suddenly had this basic idea of a boy who didn't know what he was," she said in a *School Library Journal* conversation.

Joanne was enthralled with the vision that had come to her. She immediately reached for a pen and paper to begin jotting down notes and thoughts. Unfortunately, Joanne had neither. And so, with nothing but her memory to serve her, she sat quietly and just played with the notion of characters, funny names, and story possibilities.

By the time her train stopped at Knight's Cross station in London, Joanne had the basic premise of the first Harry Potter story down. Over the next few weeks and months, Joanne put every free moment into jotting down ideas and stories centered around this imaginary boy and his adventures in a world ruled by magic. The Harry Potter files soon filled one box, then several.

Joanne continued her job at the Manchester Chamber of Commerce but took every opportunity before, during, and after work to fashion a single story line for the first Harry Potter book. In short order she came up with Harry, an orphan being raised by a cruel aunt and uncle, who after finding out he is a young wizard is whisked off to a boarding school for young wizards called Hogwarts.

Joanne would often find herself smiling as she created bits of adventure for Harry and unusual names for the characters that would populate his world. Her whole outlook improved once she was inspired by Harry. Her parents and sister noticed the change, but they knew little about what had caused it. Joanne dropped little hints about something she was working on but stopped short of revealing all. She felt that to let too much out would blunt the magic.

Joanne Kathleen Rowling was already thinking like a resident of Harry Potter's world.

But this period of good spirits would be short-lived. Her mother, who had been diagnosed with multiple sclerosis in the past year, died suddenly at the age of forty-five.

Joanne was distraught. She was well aware that her mother was ill but had no idea that MS would take her so quickly, and she felt terribly guilty that she had not been there in her mother's final hours. Her deepest regret was that she had never let her mother read any of Harry.

In her distracted state of mind, the young girl

had a tough time concentrating on work, so not too long after that, Joanne lost her job at the Manchester Chamber of Commerce.

"It was a nightmare period," sighed Joanne. She told *People* Magazine that writing about Harry was the only thing that got her through.

5

HARRY IS BORN

Joanne was in an emotional whirlwind. She had just turned twenty-six. She was once again out of work. The relationship with her boyfriend once again seemed to be going nowhere. And she was in a constantly saddened state because of the death of her mother.

The only real joy in her life was Harry Potter.

She had continued to work diligently on the book, with boxes overflowing with ideas, names, and fragments of stories. Joanne was feeling confident in what she had jotted down and began seriously contemplating writing the novel. But she was torn between living out her dream of a life dedicated to writing and the guilt she was feeling at not being like everyone else.

Joanne was thinking very hard about what her life was about and what she wanted to do with it. One of the bright spots she kept coming back to was that year she spent in Paris working as an assistant teacher. She had enjoyed it and thought she might enjoy it again. In any case, she felt she needed to do something constructive with her life.

Joanne's dreams of teaching in some far-off land finally won out. In September 1990, she announced to her family and friends that she would no longer settle for menial office work and soon accepted the offer of a job abroad, teaching English as a second language at a school in the northern Portugal town of Oporto. Joanne was both excited and frightened at the prospect of going so far away to work, but she felt that being away from home and family was the only way she would ultimately find herself.

So she packed her bags, many of which contained her notes on Harry, kissed her father and sister goodbye and promised them she would write on a regular basis. Before she knew it, she was on her way.

Although she was homesick, Joanne quickly adjusted to life in Portugal. She immediately found a comfortable apartment to live in and became well acquainted with the country, its people, and its customs. She loved walking the quaint streets, window shopping, and dealing, often unsuccessfully with the Portuguese delicacy tripe (the fatty lining of animal stomach). The people were friendly and it was sunny and warm all the time, a real contrast to the gloomy, cold weather in London. After a short while the homesickness disappeared and Joanne settled into the life of a teacher.

Joanne's students took an immediate liking to her. And when they were not making fun of her name, calling her "Rolling Stone," they would sit in rapt attention as Joanne taught them the fine art of speaking English. The transplanted Londoner was happy with the progress her students were making and proud of the good notices she had been receiving from the school superiors. She was also happy that her schedule allowed her to continue to write. "I worked afternoons and evenings," she recalled, "and so I had my mornings free to write."

Harry and his adventures at wizard school were slowly but surely coming together. The first pages of the novel were written in a wave of excitement. Joanne was discovering Harry much in the manner that her creation was discovering his magic—in short bursts of enthusiasm that often had her breaking into a spontaneous grin as the words flowed from her mind to the page.

She would chuckle as the names Hermione, Ron, Hagrid, and Dumbledore instantly became immortalized in the forms of Harry's many fantastic friends. Naming her characters was one of the most enjoyable parts about writing Harry. Long a collector of unusual names and clever when it came to creating her own, Joanne would often laugh uncontrollably when the likes of an Every Flavor Beans or a Justin Finch Fletchey would spring spontaneously to mind.

"Having a child who escapes the confines of the adult world and goes somewhere where he has power really appealed to me," the author once revealed to *The Boston Globe* of her feelings while writing the first Harry Potter book. "There's always room for a story that can transport readers to another place."

But the excitement was often tempered by the frustration of trying to get everything about Harry and his world just right. The author admitted to some tears in those early days when, in detailing Harry's life as an orphan, she was forced to deal with the passing of her own mother.

Evil was also a notion that Joanne had to deal with when creating the villainous Lord Voldemort. Rather than create bad guys typical of a children's book—noisy but not truly evil—she decided that evil in the world of Harry Potter would ring true to readers only if it was serious and its consequences fell on characters that the readers loved.

Ultimately the thing that caused Joanne the most concern was the tone of the books. From the beginning, Joanne was torn between writing the typical children's book, which often condescended to the reader, or simply writing the book that she would choose to read as an adult. Joanne chose the latter course.

Writing this book, despite the obstacles and challenges involved, was a constant joy—one that would help her through the occasional bouts of loneliness. Joanne was friendly and outgoing with her co-workers but had remained reserved and shy around men. Despite having a boyfriend at Exeter, she had never thought of herself as pretty and so had never been too concerned that the years were rolling by without the prospects of a husband or a family in her life.

But all of that changed the day Joanne Kathleen Rowling fell in love.

She and he had met by chance. He was a journalist for one of the leading television stations in Portugal. Joanne, blushing like a schoolgirl, had been instantly attracted to his bright smile and his dark good looks. As they began to date, Joanne also discovered that he was bright, sensitive, and interested in her.

Theirs was a whirlwind courtship. Within months of their meeting, Joanne and the handsome man from Portugal were married.

The first two years of their marriage were good if somewhat hectic times for the couple. Her husband's work often kept him out till all hours, and with her schedule, they often found it difficult to find private time together. Still, Joanne found inspiration in her happiness, and it showed in her enthusiasm for her work and the continued progress of Harry Potter.

What had started out as a simple tale for young children was becoming more detailed. What was intended as a book for young people was beginning to take on layers of depth equally suited for adult readers. The characters were living and breathing in a very real way; although children, they were making choices and behaving much more maturely than most characters in children's stories. And so it did not bother Joanne when Harry's adventures in Hogwarts grew, with no end in sight.

In 1992, Joanne discovered she was pregnant. The young couple was thrilled and, privately, the mother-to-be hoped that the prospect of a baby in the house would help their relationship, which had hit a rough patch.

Sadly the pressures of married life, coupled with the hormonal changes in being pregnant, soon began to weigh on Joanne. In her mind, her husband was always at work and was not showing her the kindness she had first seen in this man. Joanne would often lapse into fits of depression. There were tears. Her husband did his best to comfort her, but to no avail. Unfortunately the birth of the couple's daughter, Jessica, in 1993 did little to save the crumbling marriage.

"I was very depressed," Joanne remembered painfully in a UK News interview. "And having a newborn child made it doubly difficult. I simply felt like a nonperson. I was very low and I felt I had to achieve something."

In a matter of weeks, Joanne and her husband divorced. She has been rather secretive about her marriage, refusing to reveal the name of her husband or the actual reason for the divorce. She would only allow that "I've made my mistakes in that area. Just because you've got a good brain doesn't mean you're any better than the next person at keeping your hormones under control."

Joanne was in a terrible funk. She felt there was no reason to stay in Portugal, where the memory of her failed marriage would continue to haunt her and her prospects for any kind of life as a recently divorced woman with a child were limited. She was prepared to return to London, although the idea of returning home as a divorced single mother was not something she was looking forward to doing.

Joanne remained quiet and withdrawn in those days following the divorce. She was there for her daughter in every possible way. But she cried at the drop of a hat. And the worst part of all was that she rarely worked on the book.

In the midst of this depression, she received a telephone call from her sister, who was now quite grown and living in Edinburgh, Scotland. Di suggested that she might want to move to Edinburgh so that she could be near family while she decided what she would do next. Joanne agreed, taking Jessica, her bags, and the by now three chapters of *Harry Potter and the Sorcerer's Stone*, and hopped a train to Edinburgh. The ride to Edinburgh was long and lonely. As the weather turned from bright sunshine to dark and dreary, Joanne noted that it reflected her mood perfectly.

Although she was happy to be near her sister, once she arrived in Edinburgh, Joanne once again fell into deep despair. "I had a tiny baby, no job, and I was in a strange place," she painfully reflected in *People*.

These were not the best of times to be a single woman with a child in England and neighboring Scotland. Just a month earlier, the British prime minister, John Major, had given a speech scolding single parents for being welfare-loving freeloaders. Joanne felt particularly offended by that speech. Yes, she was a single mother with a child. But she was also a college graduate with no shortage of skills. Certainly she would be able to pull her head above water.

But as she walked around Edinburgh with Jessica, Joanne often felt the hard stares of strangers. It was as if they knew.

A guardian angel named Sean stepped forward and loaned Joanne enough money to put a deposit down on what she once called "a grotty flat." With a roof over their heads, Joanne faced the dilemma of what to do. Her heart was into finishing the Harry Potter book. But her dream was now complicated by the tiny bundle of joy asleep in her crib.

"I was terrified that I just wouldn't be able to justify to myself continuing to write," she told *School Library Journal.* "I thought it would be selfish for my daughter if I could earn a better living doing something else. If writing wasn't helping to buy new shoes, then it just felt very self-indulgent. What I was praying for was to just make enough for me to continue to write."

Christmas was fast approaching and the festivities of the season only seemed to make Joanne feel worse. She had no money for presents for her daughter and the dear friends who had been there for her. Joanne felt coming to Edinburgh had been a hasty decision, so she made plans to return to London and attempt to find another job after the first of the year.

One rainy afternoon, as she was visiting with her sister, Joanne, on an impulse, began telling her sister the story of Harry Potter, much as she had the story of Rabbit years ago. Di was immediately caught by the story and insisted that her older sister show her what she had written.

"It's possible that if she had not laughed, I would have set the whole thing to one side," recalled Joanne in the *Daily Telegraph* of that fateful moment.

"But Di did laugh."

6

DARK AND LIGHT

Making her sister laugh was the first positive experience Joanne had had in a long time. Encouraged that she might be on the right track with her book, Joanne made what she hoped would be a smart choice.

Joanne knew she would have no trouble finding another teaching job. But to do that would mean there would be no time left for writing. Finally she decided that she would finish the book in a year and try to get it published.

Joanne knew in her mind that this was a step

that, once taken, could not be taken back. She was deliberately setting herself up for a hard time. But she also realized that she had spent years sitting on the fence about her writing, to no avail. To take a chance now would not put her in any worse a predicament then she was already in.

"I thought 'What is the worst that could happen?' Every publishing company in Britain could turn me down. Big deal," she explained to the *Daily Telegraph.*

Thinking that gave the young mother strength. But she was not foolhardy in approaching this decision. Once she made her decision, "my back was up against the wall, I knew I could not afford the luxury of writer's block."

Any idea of working while she wrote went out the window when she discovered that although she was eligible to receive public assistance, she was not eligible for child care. Thus Joanne was forced into unemployment. The author would later recall that at that point she found herself in "an appalling poverty trap" from which it seemed almost impossible to emerge.

The whole process of filing for public assistance was humiliating and demoralizing. Once again she was getting those nasty looks from strangers who saw her as something to be despised.

"That was probably the lowest point in my life," she confessed to *The Boston Globe*. "My self-respect was on the floor. I didn't want Jessica to grow up this way, so she became my inspiration and writing about Harry became my safe haven."

Joanne soon discovered that many of her so-called friends were suddenly not there for her. They gave her strange looks and what conversations they had with her were strained and forced.

But the young woman was also grateful for her sister and the handful of friends who stuck with her when the attitude around town was that Joanne was nothing more than a freeloader. If she needed a few pounds to tide her over, they were there. But more important, on those days when the writing was not going well, Jessica was a handful, and she was feeling miserable, Joanne had people around who would just sit and listen as she poured her heart out.

Public assistance barely covered rent and food, so Joanne was forced to go to great lengths to save money. There were nights when there was barely enough food for mother and child, so Joanne would go to bed hungry. She could not afford even a used typewriter, and of course, even the most outdated computer was out of the question. So she would gather up scraps of paper and any pencils she could find and write out the adventures of Harry Potter in longhand.

Another problem was where to write. Her housing benefit only covered the rent on a cold, depressing one-room flat. This was hardly the place to inspire fantasy thoughts, and it was certainly not where Joanne wanted Jessica to spend the early part of her life. The struggling writer and mother put on her thinking cap and soon formulated an ingenious way to write and make her baby happy at the same time.

Every day she would put Jessica in her baby carrier and walk her around town until the child fell asleep. She would then head for one of a number of local cafés, where for the price of a cup of espresso and a glass of water, she could sit and write for a couple of hours while her daughter slept. Years later, Joanne would marvel at how much she had gotten done in those short periods of time.

One of her regular stops was the Nicolson Café,

whose co-owner, Dougal McBride, remembered how he would glance up from his work and, sure enough, there would be Joanne writing away at a corner table. "She was quite an odd sight," he remembered in *People*. "She would just push the pram with one hand and write away."

Occasionally Joanne would be too tired or the weather would be too bleak for her to risk taking Jessica out and about, so she would be forced to write in the flat. These were the times when Joanne would think that things could not get any worse.

However, through all the tough times, Joanne was buoyed up by the good cheer she was finding in writing her novel. As the pages continued to pile up, Harry Potter became her imaginary white knight, righting all the wrongs in her fantasy world that could not be fixed in her own. Her eyes would grow intense and her mouth would grow tight when she was creating the latest diabolical deed for Voldemort. And then there was wise old Dumbledore, whose every appearance in her manuscript was a time for inner joy and celebration.

"I wasn't really aware that it was a children's book," she recalled in *Newsweek* of her feelings while writing *Harry Potter and the Sorcerer's Stone*.

"I really wrote it for me. It was what I found funny and what I liked."

As she had hoped, writing *Harry Potter and the Sorcerer's Stone* was mentally and emotionally seeing her through the tough times. But as she got closer to completing the book, some of her old insecurities came flooding back. To fulfill her dream of becoming a writer, Joanne would have to risk all by sending the book out to publishers, who could dash her hopes without batting an eye.

Once she decided this was a risk worth taking, Joanne's next step was to figure out just how one went about getting published. She had heard stories about how one needed an agent in order to get one's work accepted by a book publisher. Now all she needed to do was find an agent.

Her first stop was the local library, where she found a writer's directory that listed the names and addresses of agents. Joanne pored over the directory and compiled a list of the agents she felt might be the most receptive to her book.

Harry Potter and the Sorcerer's Stone was completed early in 1994. Joanne went over the manuscript carefully, rewriting and polishing until she finally had the book exactly the way she had hoped.

Because the cost of photocopying what had turned out to be an 80,000-word book was so prohibitive, Joanne, with the aid of a cheap typewriter she had managed to purchase, typed up two copies of her novel.

Then she sent the two copies to the top two agents on her list and hoped for the best.

The year 1994 became a turning point in Joanne's life. She had applied for and had received a grant from the Scottish Arts Council. The money was enough to allow Joanne to get proper child care for Jessica during the day. Encouraged by this, she began looking for work and soon found a job in Edinburgh as a teacher of French at the Leth Academy and, later, at the Moray House Training College. True to her word, a year to the day that Joanne pulled into Edinburgh, penniless, she was now self-sufficient and off welfare.

Joanne Rowling was feeling reborn.

In her spare time, Joanne continued to play around with Harry Potter and had soon come up with a story line for a second book. She was hoping against hope that a second book would be possible. But thus far, there was nothing to convince her that it would ever come to pass.

"I had no idea truthfully what kind of reception it would get," she explained in *School Library Journal*. "If indeed it would ever get published, because I never looked to publish before. I knew how difficult it would be and I was a completely unknown writer."

One day a letter arrived in the mail. Joanne could tell immediately it was from one of the agents she had sent a copy of Harry to. She was thrilled to get a response. But as she tore open the envelope . . .

"I assumed it was a rejection note," she recalled in the *Daily Telegraph*. "But inside the envelope there was a letter saying 'Thank you. We would be pleased to represent your manuscript on an exclusive basis.' It was the best letter of my life. I read it eight times."

Christopher Little was an all-business, bottom-line kind of person. But this unsolicited manuscript by a totally unknown writer had touched him. It was very well written, the story was entertaining and, like Joanne, he sensed that *Harry Potter and the Sorcerer's Stone* was not merely a children's book.

Upon meeting her, Christopher Little was also

impressed with her enthusiasm and her struggles against formidable odds to get the book written. He liked her grasp of reality. From his experience, Mr. Little knew that most children's authors struggle to make £2,000 ($4,000) a year and that they rarely wind up being well known.

"When I went into this, my agent said to me, 'I don't want you going away from this meeting thinking you're going to make a fortune,' " she reported to *School Library Journal.* "Then I said to him, 'I know I'm not going to make any money out of it. I know I'm not going to be famous.' All I ever wanted was for somebody to publish Harry so I could go to bookshops and see it."

Mr. Little began sending out *Harry Potter and the Sorcerer's Stone* to some of the biggest publishers in England. And as he had predicted, it was a long, hard road to being published. Before long, the first of a seemingly endless stream of rejections arrived at her agent's door. Some of the reasons given for not wanting to publish the book were that it was too long, too slow, or too literary. Joanne was disappointed but was encouraged by Mr. Little's assessment that the book was too good not to be picked up at some point.

Joanne went about her business of being a mother and a teacher and tried to put the chilly reception to Harry out of her thoughts. But during the next year, she would often find herself daydreaming about spying her book in the front window of the local bookshop. During those moments she would find herself smiling at the events in her life that had brought her to this moment.

In 1996, *Harry Potter and the Sorcerer's Stone* finally found a home with British publisher Bloomsbury Press. Joanne was beside herself with joy when she heard the news. "It was comparable only to having my daughter."

True to Mr. Little's prediction, Bloomsbury offered the modest amount of £2,000.

"That was totally okay with me," she once revealed of her reaction to Bloomsbury's acceptance of Harry. "All I wanted was to be able to support myself writing so I wouldn't have to give it up."

As often happens in the publishing industry, word of mouth about the merit of *Harry Potter and the Sorcerer's Stone* was good. Within months of Bloomsbury's purchase of the book, inquiries from publishers all over the world began pouring in.

In 1997, the overwhelming interest in this children's book by an unknown writer had reached such a level that an auction was arranged at the time of the annual Bologna, Italy, Book Fair (an annual book industry get-together in which foreign rights to books are sold). Joanne had been so thrilled at the prospect of Harry being published in her native England that she had paid only scant attention to what had been going on elsewhere in the world.

But she laughed when she recalled in *Salon* magazine the night her telephone rang around eight. It was Mr. Little calling long distance from New York.

"He said there was an auction taking place. An auction? I thought 'Sotheby's, Christie's [famous antiques auction house]?' Antiques? What is this all about? Then I realized that it was my book that was being auctioned off."

At that very moment, thousands of miles away in a crowded room at the Bologna Book Fair, editorial director Arthur A. Levine was about to take the biggest gamble of his life. The bidding on *Harry Potter and the Sorcerer's Stone* had been intense and the amounts being put up for the U.S. rights had already reached astronomical heights.

Levine, a spirited man with a ready smile, was about to make a bid that could change his life forever.

"It's a scary thing when you keep bidding and the stakes are getting higher and higher," said Levine in *The New York Times*. "It's one thing to say I love this first novel by this unknown woman in Scotland and I want to publish it. It's another thing as the bidding goes higher. Do you love it this much? Do you love it at $50,000? At $70,000?"

The reason for Levine's concern was that the bidding was back to him and he was faced with the decision of offering an unheard-of bid of $100,000. "I had never paid so much for an acquisition before. It was a great risk. If people believe in you and you flop, then you walk out on the plank and plunge."

Little called Joanne again at ten that same evening. "He said I should get ready because a Mr. Levine of the Scholastic Press would pay a six-figure sum for the book and would be ringing me in a little bit. I nearly died."

The tension mounted in Joanne's tiny Edinburgh flat. She was excited and scared all at the same time. She had hoped, under ideal circumstances, that a modest U.S. sale would allow her to continue to write and teach on a part-time basis. But, she reasoned, things seemed to be moving much faster than anybody had expected.

The telephone rang promptly at eleven P.M. At the other end of the line, Levine was determined not to put any undue pressure on his new author. But his voice was shaking with excitement as he said hello.

"I called her very late," he told *The New York Times*, "and we had a very nice conversation. I said 'Don't be scared,' and she said, 'Thanks, I am.' And we both said now that we've paid this much, we had to concentrate on making the book work."

It was well past midnight when Joanne, after checking on her sleeping daughter, finally went to bed. "But I couldn't sleep. On one level, I was obviously delighted," she told a *Salon* magazine reporter. "But most of me was just frozen in terror."

7

HARRY CONQUERS THE WORLD

Joanne had good reason to be fearful in the weeks following her big signing with Scholastic Books.

The amount of money involved was so unheard of in children's book circles that the book publishing gossip was that Arthur Levine and Scholastic had taken leave of their senses. Many doomsayers predicted that no matter how good the book was, it would certainly not make anywhere near enough to earn back the massive advance.

Joanne's agent and Arthur Levine assured her

that Scholastic Books was not in the habit of laying out huge amounts of money for books they felt would fail. Joanne was not completely convinced. But that was only part of her concern.

Word of this author who had landed an advance unheard of for a children's book had quickly spread around the world. The normally shy woman was now being deluged with requests for interviews and her picture was appearing in newspapers and magazines. And this was before her book was even published in Great Britain.

If it had been up to her, Joanne would have done no publicity for the book at all. But she felt a strong sense of loyalty to those who had taken this chance with her, so she said yes to every request.

"The stakes had seemed to have gone up a lot," she told an interviewer in 1999 of those exciting days following her signing with Scholastic Press in the United States. "I attracted a lot of publicity for which I was totally unprepared."

Joanne was not big on change, and the idea of doing interviews in stuffy hotel rooms and television studios ran contrary to her nature. So when she started entertaining the press, she would gently insist that, whenever possible, interviews be done at her familiar table in the Nicholson Café.

When these interviews took place, a crowd of waiters and waitresses would stand on the periphery listening. They would smile as Joanne told how she would sit at this very table and write under the most trying of situations. Many of them had served her when she was down on her luck. Now they were as proud as they could possibly be that their regular customer was a well-known author.

Initially, she was not comfortable doing interviews. Joanne was not always smooth in her responses and worried about the kind of impression she was making. But she knew only how to be honest, and the press were going to make of that what they would.

Much of that early publicity put Joanne on the defensive. In many newspaper and magazine interviews, the reporters painted a picture of Joanne as a penniless, divorced single mother living on welfare and writing at her leisure in cafés. She had no problem with the accuracy, and yes, it was true. But she felt "knocked sideways" by the negative image it presented of her and the fact that it was forcing her to relive what she considered one of the saddest moments of her life.

Joanne was quick to clarify that she had been gainfully employed since 1990, when she started writing Harry, and that the only reason she had to go on welfare was that the system in Edinburgh would not allow for child care. And then, she insisted, it was only for the year that she was completing the book.

As *Harry Potter and the Sorcerer's Stone* was going through the publishing process in England, Joanne found that there was one more compromise she was being asked to make. The publishers, fearful that a book with a woman's name on the cover might not attract young boys, asked if Joanne would mind if she were listed as J. K. Rowling. Joanne thought it was an odd request but saw no harm in going along with the notion.

Harry Potter and the Sorcerer's Stone was published in England in 1997. The book was an immediate smash, selling more than 150,000 copies in a matter of months. Reviewers fell over themselves in praise of the book.

One critic stated: "The book is an unassailable stand for the power of fresh, innovative storytelling." Another offered: "Rowling's ability to put a fantastic spin on sports, student rivalry, and eccentric faculty contributes to the humor, charm, and delight of her utterly captivating story."

By the end of the year, *Harry Potter and the Sorcerer's Stone* had gathered up a number of prestigious book awards, including the Nestlé Smarties Book Prize, the Federation of Children's Books Group Award and the British Book Awards Children's Book of the Year. Into 1998, the book had reached the total of a half million copies sold, an unheard-of number for a children's book.

Joanne was thrilled and more than a bit amused at what was happening with Harry. She was hard-pressed to answer the question she often asked as a child. Why? "I suppose it's mainly word of mouth," she offered of the book's success in the London *Guardian*. "I think children just tell one another about it."

But she did have a good laugh at the notion that the reason so many books were being sold was because a good many of them were being snapped up by adults just as eager to read the adventures of Harry as their children. As an example, she cited a story she had heard from a friend who had seen a man in a suit on a train reading a copy behind his newspaper.

"I had not aimed the books at children," she once said. "I only wrote them for me."

With the money from her U.S. book deal and another eight countries rolling in, Joanne was slowly beginning to adjust to the idea of not being poor. Oh, it did not come in one big gulp. She agonized for a long time whether to purchase a $100 coat so that she would look proper for her television appearances.

But with the success of *Harry Potter and the Sorcerer's Stone* in England and the American edition due out shortly, Joanne decided it was time to leave poverty behind her. The first thing she did was rent a house in Edinburgh. Nothing fancy. Just well-lighted rooms, heat, and comfortable furniture. However, for Joanne, it was pure heaven and relief. "I no longer have the constant worry of whether Jessica will outgrow a pair of shoes before I've got the money for the next pair," she sighed in a *Daily Telegraph* story.

Joanne was already hard at work on the follow-up to *Harry Potter and the Sorcerer's Stone* before the first book was published. So when she was not handling the increasing demand for interviews or tending to her daughter, Joanne was turning out pages of what would ultimately be titled *Harry Potter and the Chamber of Secrets*. But while she was now able to afford a computer and Jessica was of an age where she was spending part of the day in preschool, little of Joanne's approach to writing had changed.

Every day, after kissing her daughter goodbye, Joanne would walk down to Nicholson's Café, pull up a chair at a table facing out an upstairs window, pull out paper and a pen, and begin writing. The first time she did this after her first book had been accepted, the waiter, who had served her regularly when she was down and out, did a double take when she asked for a menu. One reason for continuing the routine was that Joanne felt lonely at the prospect of sitting in her house, by herself, in front of a computer.

"Writing and cafés are strongly linked in my brain," she recently proclaimed to the press. "I still write in longhand. I like physically shuffling around with papers."

Harry Potter and the Chamber of Secrets was almost complete and ready for publication when the U.S. edition of *Harry Potter and the Sorcerer's*

Stone was brought out in August 1998. The British mania for Harry Potter was soon duplicated in the United States as children and adults fell in love with Harry and his adventures.

In short order, editions of Joanne's first book were coming out in nearly thirty other countries. Joanne would have a giggle at the different languages and, in some cases, the different covers her story was published with. As each new edition was released, her happiness increased.

Publishers on both sides of the Atlantic were now convinced that Harry Potter was no fluke, so contracts were quickly drawn up that would have Joanne writing a total of seven Harry Potter books in the coming years. Joanne was thrilled. Then she was scared to death.

In a practical sense, the longevity of the contract meant she would never want for anything for her daughter or herself. But there was also what she described as "a few weeks of terror" as she contemplated whether she could write the remainder of the books with the same enthusiasm now that the whole world was looking over her shoulder.

To relieve the fear of writer's block, Joanne sat down and plotted out the remaining five Harry

Potter books. She was painstaking in figuring out the story lines, the specific elements of each adventure, and the important message that readers young and old would take away from each book. At the end of this plotting session, Joanne emerged confident in her ability to finish Harry Potter's education.

"And I finally realized what the most important thing for me was," she stated in *The Boston Globe*. "I love writing these books. I don't think anyone could enjoy reading them more than I enjoy writing them."

Harry Potter and the Chamber of Secrets was published in July 1998 and, like its predecessor, was an immediate sensation all over the world. In Great Britain alone, the book outsold the latest novels by adult writers John Grisham and Tom Clancy.

Joanne continued to be amazed at the way people had taken Harry Potter and his world into their hearts and minds. But the writer was also finding that having bestselling books was also beginning to complicate her life. Already well into writing the third book, *Harry Potter and the Prisoner of Azkaban*, Joanne was finding that she had less time to write because of interviews, book signings, and the odd lectures and school appearances.

Joanne was a good sport when it came to things like that. In the case of the book signings and appearances at schools, she loved the idea of actually meeting with the children who were reading her books. "As an ex-teacher, it's just so liberating to go in front of a class simply to entertain them and it's great when they've read the books and can quote you passages and know the characters," she said in *The Guardian*.

But there were also those days when things did not go according to plan and Joanne found herself overwhelmed to the point of tears. During what seemed like an endless round of promotional duties surrounding the release of *Harry Potter and the Chamber of Secrets*, Joanne was having trouble checking out of a London hotel. At first the hotel would not allow her to check out because there was no record of her name in the computer. Finally a hotel manager found her name but insisted that she could not leave until she paid her bill. This upset the normally unflappable Joanne because she knew that her publisher had already paid the bill. With the hotel fiasco finally straightened out, she hopped in a taxi, already late for an interview. Halfway there, Joanne realized that she had left the hotel without her purse.

It was all too much. Joanne burst into tears, startling the cabdriver.

However, most days her good humor and sunny outlook got Joanne through the difficulty of being in the public eye. She felt incredibly fortunate to be in this position because it had come as a result of her unwillingness to give up on her dream. So, yes, she would give interviews and talk to people about Harry until the cows came home.

But at the end of the day she would happily race home to comfort Jessica. As she held her young daughter and asked about her day at school, Joanne was proud—proud that as her mother, she was able to provide Jessica with security and a good life.

And if there was time, Joanne would walk down to Nicholson's Café, where she might find a few moments to write. She would sometimes order the usual espresso and water. But just as often she would also pick up the menu . . .

And think about getting something to eat.

8

HARRY EVER AFTER

Harry Potter and the Prisoner of Azkaban was released late in 1998. The mania for Harry continued as the book immediately followed its predecessors to the top of the world's bestseller lists.

Reporters once again came around, hoping the quiet author of these fantastic adventures would have a reason for Harry Potter's continued success. And once again Joanne found it hard to come up with an answer that did not have the words "shocked and amazed" somewhere in it.

Happily, Joanne was more than willing to try. "I am still stunned that I went from being an unknown writer on the breadline to having my books at the top of the charts. It's truly amazing," she would regularly tell reporters.

But all the news was not good. A number of religious groups had decided that Harry Potter books were promoting evil thoughts and ideas. Many of these groups sent letters to newspapers protesting the books, and in some cases, they tried to get the books removed from libraries and bookstores.

Joanne was upset by their actions but chose to ignore them. Eventually the storm of protest passed.

Joanne celebrated New Year's Eve 1999 quietly with a small group of friends. At the stroke of midnight, she toasted her good fortune and her good friends. She could only imagine what the upcoming year would offer.

A resolution was not long in coming. Nobody had ever referred to Joanne as a workaholic. But as fast as the new Harry books were coming out, one had to wonder if Joanne did anything but write. She repeatedly stated that writing was the thing she most liked to do. However, she did decide that she owed it to herself and Jessica to get away every once in a while. So she began traveling, taking short jaunts to neighboring countries that would allow Jessica and her to see the sights and get away from the distractions that were always a phone call away in Edinburgh.

It came as no surprise that Hollywood was soon wild about Harry as well. Moviemakers immediately saw the possibilities of Harry Potter as a movie. No fewer than a dozen film studios were actively pursuing the rights to turn Harry Potter into a full-length motion picture. Once again, Joanne was hanging by the telephone as Christopher Little relayed the latest messages regarding a film contract. But the negotiation of film deals, unlike that of book deals, tends to drag on for a long time, so Joanne was content to go about the business of writing the fourth installment of Harry Potter.

With two books out in the same year, Joanne was given more time to turn out this latest adventure. There had been some concern by the publishers that writing two books literally back-to-back might have put a bit of a strain on their favorite author. However, Joanne was nothing if not anxious, after the seemingly endless round of press and publicity, to get back to creating another exciting Harry Potter adventure for her legion of fans.

The routine remained pretty much the same. Although her notoriety had made the Nicholson Café a sudden tourist attraction, and Joanne would occasionally find herself feeling self-conscious at being gawked at by people who had come to watch her work, she would still find time to sit and work there a few hours just about every day. But out of necessity, she was also working in other cafés and pubs, which she wisely refused to name.

Wherever she went, the writing continued to go smoothly. The characters had become like a second family to her. She knew what would work and what would appear false. Creating new names for her otherworldly characters was always a joy. But Joanne had to admit that with this book, things were beginning to change. Harry and the other characters were now well into their teen years. She felt it was time to have Harry discover girls.

This was an exciting turn of events for Joanne, one that allowed her to revisit her own adolescence as a blueprint for how Harry should react the first time he notices a girl as something other than a good buddy. Harry was never boring, but now there was an extra bit of excitement that would have her snatching up her pen and paper at every opportunity.

Shortly before the turn of the New Year 2000, Joanne, with Jessica by her side, boarded an airplane at London's Heathrow Airport, headed for the United States on a three-week book tour. These were exciting times for Joanne. She had heard about how well the first three books had done in America, but she was anxious to meet with her readers face-to-face and to see the joy and excitement they had for her work in their eyes.

At each and every stop on this cross-country tour, Joanne was very much the teacher in her dealings with the thousands of fans who lined up to see her. She would encourage them to read and write as often as possible. She would chuckle at the inevitable question on how to pronounce her name before saying, "It's Roe-ling, not Row-ling." The woman of simple tastes even got to like the rock-star treatment she was getting with limo rides and big security at every stop. The look on Joanne's face was worth a thousand words. But only one was really necessary . . .

Joy.

The year 2000 would bring continued success for Joanne. *Harry Potter and the Goblet of Fire* was in place for a July 8, 2000, publication date. It was also announced during this period that Warner Bros. had captured the rights to make the movie version of *Harry Potter and the Sorcerer's Stone*. Originally the studio had stated that Steven Spielberg was interested in directing the film. But the director would later bow out of the project, saying "My directorial interests were taking me in another direction." Eventually the studio made its choice and assigned a talented director, Chris Columbus, and a screenwriter, Steven Kloves, to adapt Joanne's fantasy world to the screen.

Joanne agreed to the Warner Bros. offer on the condition that she would have input into the screenplay and that the movie would be live action rather than animation. But as the studio officially announced that Harry Potter would be in theaters in the summer of 2001, she had to admit to being nervous about the prospect of seeing Harry on the big screen. "It's actually a mixture of excitement and nervousness," she offered upon hearing the good news, in a Web site chat. "I do think Harry would make a great film. But obviously I do feel protective toward the characters I've lived with so long."

In March, director Columbus flew to Scotland, where he and Joanne met. Both came away from the meeting enthusiastic about the film. "I'm terribly excited," said Columbus in the *Los Angeles Times*. "My oldest daughter, Eleanor, who is ten, got me into the books over a year ago. Between my four kids and their friends, I've heard a lot about what this movie should be and how I could ruin it if I cut this or that scene. I won't let anyone down. It will be a faithful adaptation."

Joanne was also in good spirits about her sudden involvement in the movie business. "I'm more involved than I thought I would be. I can't wait to see how they will pull off a Quidditch game."

The publicity campaign for the release of *Harry Potter and the Goblet of Fire* reached massive proportions as the days counted down to the official publication date. At this point, Joanne was not looking forward to answering a lot of the same questions yet again; she had in recent months started saying no to all but the most important outlets just so she would have time to write.

Her publishers took the hint and, in late spring,

announced that Joanne would do one ninety-minute interview session in London and that would be it. Soon journalists from all over the world were flying in for the opportunity to ask the world's most popular author questions about her new book and her life in general.

Joanne was a bit nervous at the prospect of facing so many reporters at the same time and was concerned that this massive press conference would get out of control. Much of the press conference turned out to be predictable. There were the usual questions concerning why Harry had proven to be so popular, her struggles in Edinburgh, and how she was coping with success. Joanne fielded them with ease and responded, often with humor, concisely. But there were some surprise announcements along the way.

Joanne revealed that an important character would die in the fourth book and that Harry would develop his first crush on a girl. The author also offered that in the fifth book readers would finally discover why Harry continues to spend his summers with the frightful Dursleys.

The secretive author also offered that Harry's parents would not return and that she had decided long ago that magic could not bring back the dead. But she did hint that Harry's parents would continue to be an important part of future books.

She left the press conference relieved that the hard part of writing was once again behind her. Now she could get back to the fun part . . .

The writing itself.

Joanne would continue to be anxious as July 8 got closer and closer. At this point, nobody was betting against the fact that *Harry Potter and the Goblet of Fire* would do as well, if not better, than her previous three books. But Joanne was never one to take anything for granted.

Finally the date had arrived and Joanne crossed her fingers as her latest Harry Potter adventure went on sale in England and the United States at the same time. Within hours, the first reports began to come in. Bookstores were selling out of copies in a matter of minutes and were already on the telephone to reorder. Within days, the book was high up on the bestseller charts around the world. Joanne heaved a sigh of relief at the news.

Because the magic of Harry Potter was still there.

Joanne moved through the end of summer in a

state of grace. She was already hard at work at the next Harry book. She was happy and healthy, and she had a wonderful daughter to boot.

But with the beginning of book number five, the end was now in sight. Harry Potter would graduate from his seven years of schooling at Hogwarts some time around the year 2003. And although she would occasionally tease about never saying never when asked if she would follow Harry off to college, the author has remained adamant that Harry Potter will end with book number seven.

She has admitted to feeling sad at the idea that Harry will someday end and feels that it will be a "bereavement" when she has written the last line on the final page. But she insists that "there will be no Harry Potter's midlife crisis or Harry Potter as an old wizard."

But as she closes in on the end of the year 2000, Joanne could not be happier. Her life has exceeded her expectations. She has a beautiful daughter and she is making a living doing what she loves to do. And she is not sad at the fact that there is no man in her life. Her feeling on that topic is that if Mr. Perfect were to come along, she would be thrilled.

"But it's not my top priority," she told *Salon* magazine. "Right now my life is very fulfilled."

While her future after Harry Potter is still up in the air, the author knows that it will center on writing. It is all she knows, and she feels putting pen to paper is necessary for her. Joanne once admitted that "I don't feel normal when I haven't written for a while."

Joanne has hinted many times that her next step after Harry would be to write more adult novels. But she is honest enough to realize that she will probably never write anything as popular as Harry, and that is all right with her.

"I will have lived with Harry for thirteen years and I know I'll probably have to take some time off to grieve. But then I'll be on with the next book."

What that will be is anybody's guess, including Joanne's. But she knows where she will go for inspiration. "I might just get on another train."

9

TOUCHED BY
AN ANGEL

wo dramas were unfolding in July 1999.

In her Edinburgh, Scotland, home, Joanne was working day and night in an attempt to finish *Harry Potter and the Goblet of Fire*. She was refusing all interview requests and avoiding any distractions that would keep her from finishing the long anticipated fourth adventure of Harry Potter.

The fame and celebrity status that had grown up around Joanne had caused her to alter her writing routine. Her phone rang constantly, interrupting her quiet time in the room in her house that doubled as her office and writing room. And though she continued to spend much of each day writing at the table of her favorite outdoor restaurant, Nicholson's, word had gotten out and she was often interrupted by sightseers requesting a photo or an autograph. Eventually she began writing in other restaurants around town in an attempt to find the time to finally finish *Goblet of Fire*. Joanne was finding that dealing with fame was not always easy.

At the same time, in Toronto, Canada, nine-year-old Natalie McDonald was dying of leukemia.

Natalie was the ultimate Harry Potter fan. She lived and breathed Joanne's stories from the beginning, and it was Harry Potter's flights of fantasy that had helped the young girl cope with her pain and her illness. A family friend, Annie Kidder, wanted to do something special to make Natalie's last days a bit more pleasant and felt that hearing from her favorite author would make the young girl deliriously happy.

Annie found the address for Joanne's London publisher and sent a series of letters, E-mails, and faxes, explaining Natalie's dire situation and requesting some kind of response from the author. The people in the publishing office were touched by the sincerity of Annie's messages and, despite Joanne's strict order not to be disturbed as she raced to complete *Harry Potter and the Goblet of Fire*, they believed this heartfelt request was something she would want to respond to. Finally the latest letter from Annie Kidder was forwarded to Joanne's Edinburgh home.

Joanne was not there to receive it.

After an intense period of writing, Joanne felt she needed a break and so had decided, in mid July, to take a short vacation in Spain. Annie's letter had arrived the day after Joanne left. When she returned from her holiday, the first thing she read was the letter from Annie. She was touched and saddened at her young fan's illness and immediately felt compelled to do something to help.

"But I had a bad feeling that I was too late," she told *Maclean's*.

Joanne called Annie Kidder but she was not at home. She instantly dashed off a long letter and E-mailed a copy to Natalie and her mother, Valerie. The E-mail arrived on August 4, 1999.

Sadly, Joanne would later discover that her message had arrived too late. Natalie had died on August 3.

But Annie would recall Joanne's kind words in that letter. She treated the dying young girl with respect and lovingly talked about her books and characters. In the body of that letter, Joanne also revealed the story and secrets of *Harry Potter and the Goblet of Fire*, a full eleven months before the book was to be released.

This might have been the end of a very sad story.

But Joanne had other ideas. The author, heartbroken by her inability to bring comfort to the young child's final days, had been so moved by Natalie and her life struggles and devotion to Harry Potter that she decided to honor the girl she had never met but writing her into a passage of *Harry Potter and the Goblet of Fire*. And so on page 159 of *Goblet of Fire*, Joanne created a scene in which the sorting hat sends first-year student Natalie McDonald to Harry's Gryffindor house. This would be the only time Joanne would ever use a real person's name in a Harry Potter book.

After receiving Joanne's letter to her daughter, Natalie's mother, Valerie, wrote back to thank the author for her efforts on behalf of her daughter. Joanne was touched by Valerie's letter, and a regular correspondence began between the two women. As the letters went back and forth between Canada and Scotland, Joanne found that she had discovered in Valerie a kindred spirit, someone, who like Joanne, had experienced the death of a loved one, and who felt strongly about the importance and challenges of motherhood.

As the time for publication of *Harry Potter and the Goblet of Fire* neared, Joanne and Valerie agreed to meet in England to cement their relationship face to face. And so in July 2000, Valerie, her husband, and two other daughters traveled to England to meet with Joanne.

Joanne was unsure how this meeting would go. She had always been a very private person and this kind of friendship was out of character for her. But the kindness and love expressed in their letters had found a special place in Joanne's heart and so she felt comfortable about meeting this woman.

The meeting between the two women was a joyous, bittersweet time. There were hugs all around, tears were shed in joy and happiness in the memory of a child whom Valerie had lost and Joanne had never known but, in a very spiritual sense, had come to know.

It was during their London visit that Valerie and her family, on a sightseeing excursion around the city on the London tube, discovered Joanne's secret memorial to Natalie. To pass the time on the tube, Valerie began reading *Harry Potter and the Goblet of Fire* to her daughters. One can only imagine the surprise when she turned to page 159 and discovered how Joanne had chosen to honor the memory of Natalie.

Natalie McDonald was in heaven. But in the heart and mind of Joanne Kathleen Rowling, she would forever live in Hogwarts.

10

THE HOGWARTS
EXPRESS

Alight blue car pulled to a stop at London's King's Cross Station on July 8, 2000. Inside, Joanne was still rubbing the sleep from her eyes at the early morning wakeup. She was already missing her daughter, Jessica, who would be sleeping soundly in the home of her sister, Di, as she prepared to catch a train.

Looking outside, Joanne saw a scene of total chaos. A literal army of photographers and reporters had lined the railway station entrance, television cameras jockeying for a good position, people being pushed and shoved every which way. Beyond the cluster of press people and behind a barricade stood more than three hundred children and their bewildered parents, who had braved the cold weather and the early hour for a chance to see their favorite author.

Sadly, while the photographers and reporters were given free rein to move wherever they wanted, the children were being kept in that one spot, making even a glimpse of Joanne all but impossible.

As she emerged from the car, a fresh-off-the-presses copy of *Harry Potter and the Goblet of Fire* clutched in her hands, a shout went up from a group of photographers, who begged: "Give us a wave, Jo!" For Joanne, it was a bit early in the morning for this sort of thing. But after a moment's hesitation, she rolled her eyes, presented a half smile–half grimace to the photographers, and offered up a halfhearted wave as the flashbulbs exploded around her like lightning.

"It's rather mad isn't it?" she joked with photographers as they snapped away. "I'd really like to talk to some children if I ever manage to finish with you lot."

With that, Joanne made a break through the

crowd and instinctively made for the children. Sadly, she was intercepted by public relations people and ushered back toward the waiting cameras.

"I'm sorry," she yelled at the children as she was hustled away. "I'm not allowed."

Surrounded by personal assistants and representatives of her British publishing company, Joanne made her way through the station and to Platform 9¾. Where she came face to face with The Queen of Scots which, for the occasion, had been made over into a real life incarnation of The Hogwarts Express. The train, an old-fashioned, red, steam-powered engine not unlike the fictional train that takes Harry Potter to the School of Witchcraft and Wizardry, is pouring smoke out of its towering stack. Behind it, an observation car, a dining car, and a sleeping car are rapidly filling up with people. Joanne stops in front of the train and smiles gamely one last time for the photographers and steps aboard.

The Hogwarts Express will be Joanne's home for the next four days.

As part of a massive publicity stunt to kick off the official publication of *Harry Potter and the Goblet of Fire*, Joanne agreed to go on a train tour, beginning at London's King's Cross station and ending at Perth, Scotland. The train would make stops at train stations along the way and Joanne would sign books for a limited number of children, whose names were chosen in drawings sponsored by bookstores at bookstores, museums, or the train stations at each stop. It was a grand idea to help promote her new book, but Joanne saw the train ride as something much more important—an opportunity to meet her young readers face to face.

"I love meeting the child readers," she said in *Maclean's*. "They ask the best questions. The children talk about the characters as though they're mutual friends I happen to know a bit better."

Promptly at 11:27 A.M., the train began to slowly pull out of the station amid the crush of television cameras, news reporters and the number of children who had awakened as early as 4 A.M. just so they could get to the station and see their favorite author off. Joanne sensed her young fans' disappointment and stuck her head out the window and waved at the children.

"Oh God. I'm sorry. I'm sorry," she called out to the children. "It was nice meeting you all."

Joanne was saddened at what she considered

the shabby treatment her young fans received, and at the same time, more than a bit overwhelmed by the enormous interest in her latest book. She vowed to make it up to the children at the first opportunity. As for all the cameras going off and the reporters treating every word that tumbled out of her mouth as gold, she did not know if she would ever get used to that.

Joanne took a quick tour of the train. She immediately fell in love with the dining car, whose plush brocade furnishings seemed fit for royalty and would offer her a wonderful view of the countryside as the train flew past. The dining car was decked out in antique elegance, a finery reserved for the kings and queens these cars had once carried. And, at the end of the day, the sleeping car would assuredly provide her pleasant dreams.

Amid darkening clouds and the promise of a summer rain, the train left Knights Crossing and pulled steadily out of London, the cars beginning the steady rock and rattles that would be the trip's constant companion. Not too long after leaving Knights Crossing, the steam engine unceremoniously broke down and a modern-day diesel was recruited to tow the older train for the remainder of the trip.

Inside, Joanne had made herself comfortable and was beginning the first of many interviews with the members of the press on board. It was a time of reflection as she once again told the story of how Harry came to be, the latest news regarding the Harry Potter movie, and the behind-the-scenes stories of writing *Harry Potter and the Goblet of Fire*. And there were many new revelations. For the first time, Joanne candidly revealed that she had, in fact, been late completing the book, due in part to having scrapped the manuscript and started over when she realized that her presentation of the story and the characters was not consistent with the three previous books and would not reach the conclusion she wanted. And, for the first of many times, she tried to express her reaction to the continued worldwide popularity of the Harry Potter books.

"I can't explain it," she offered a reporter from the *New York Times* at one point. "I don't have an answer. I just write what I wanted to write. I write what amuses me. It's totally for myself. I never in my wildest dreams expected this popularity."

The first stop for The Hogwarts Express was a mid-afternoon signing at Didicot Railway Centre in the town of Didicot. That first night the train chugged into the Kidderminster Station in the Severen Valley. Joanne appreciated the logistics of the tour. The plan included big and small cities alike, and the trip was reminding Joanne of the old days when she traveled everywhere by train.

On the second day of the tour, the fantasy train stopped in the cities of Manchester and York. By the third day, the train had left Newcastle and had crossed over into Scotland and into her hometown of Edinburgh, where Joanne was greeted as a hometown hero.

It was the same at every stop. The train would pull into the station and Joanne would either be whisked away to a local bookstore, where she would meet a selected group of her fans and sign their books. Or, more often than not, she would meet and greet her admirers in the train station.

As always, Joanne put on her best smiling face despite the frequent early-morning stops on the schedule and the fact she readily had admitted in *Reader's Digest* that "I'm really not a morning person." But nothing, including the fact that she was already missing Jessica, would stop her from being the embodiment of all her fans fantasies . . . even if only for a moment.

And at each stop, there were wondrous stories of the lengths that many of her fans went to get an audience with Joanne. A twelve-year-old boy won a coveted ticket to meet Joanne by winning a complex Harry Potter trivia quiz. Upon hearing that a London bookstore was giving away tickets, one persistent girl awoke at 4 A.M. and was in line outside the bookstore at 6:30 A.M., hours before the store was due to open. Still another young girl had sadly thought she had lost out on the drawing, but was miraculously rewarded with a ticket when one of the original winners gave up his ticket to attend a school athletic event.

And at each stop along the tour, the reaction from the children was always the same . . . shock, delight, amazement, and a sudden inability to speak. To finally get to meet the creator of their fantasies was, according to the description of the scene by an *Entertainment Weekly* reporter, "deliriously mind boggling."

The excitement generated by Joanne's appearances was best summed up by one ten-year-old who emerged from a brief meeting with Joanne and exclaimed, "Am I allowed to faint now?"

Finally, on the fourth day, The Hogwarts Express pulled into the railroad station in Perth, Scotland. Joanne was both relieved and excited that this was the last stop on her book tour. She greeted this last group of anxious fans with a broad smile and a respectful attitude. As she signed this last batch of books, she was able to ask each child about what they liked about the books and who their favorite character was. At one point, a child was asked to pose with Joanne for a photograph. The child appeared a bit nervous at being pushed into the spotlight, but Joanne calmed him when she jokingly said, "Pretend like you're thrilled to see me."

Finally, with the last book signed, Joanne got into a car for a sixty-minute ride back to her house in Edinburgh. During the ride back, she looked out the window at the passing scenery and reflected on the turn her life had taken. In the past year, she had been named by the prestigious *Forbes* Magazine one of the top twenty-five most powerful celebrities in the world. In June 2000, she had made a quick trip to Dartmouth College in New Hampshire, where she received her first honorary degree. But easily a high point came to Joanne in the past month when she was summoned to Buckingham Palace, where she was awarded The Order Of The British Empire by the royal family.

There were other, more personal memories to relive. There was the joy in watching Jessica grow into quite the wonderful young girl, turning six and entering school. Because she did not feel Jessica had been old enough to comprehend the world of Harry Potter, Joanne had decided that she would not begin to read the stories to her until her daughter turned age seven. But what she discovered is that the children in her daughter's class were already quite familiar with her work and so they were constantly coming up to Jessica and asking her questions about Harry that she did not have the answers to.

"She didn't have an idea what they were all about," Joanne once explained to *Entertainment Weekly*. "And I just thought, 'I'm excluding her from this huge part of my life, and it's making her an outsider.' So I read them to her and she became completely Harry Potter obsessed."

And there were the obvious changes that had taken place in her own life as the result of the worldwide popularity of Harry Potter. She had more money than she ever dreamed of having. But she spent wisely, insuring a wonderful life for Jessica and herself. But the added attention was not always welcome. Before her Harry Potter books became a global sensation, Joanne was still able to move about Edinburgh without being recognized and could still spend hours writing at her favorite café, while listening to good music and sipping from a seemingly bottomless cup of coffee.

But with the publication of the third Harry Potter book, *Harry Potter and the Prisoner of Azkaban*, Joanne began to notice an increasing lack of privacy. With her writing habits now well publicized, she soon began to be the center of attention as she would write at an outside table of a cafe. And although people were always pleasant when approaching her, it would often conflict with what she insisted on being her ideal writing day.

"In an ideal day, I'll work six to ten hours," she told a Knight Ridder News Service reporter. "But now I'm fighting to get the time to write. I use cafes like offices and I try to get away from the house whenever possible."

But with her notoriety, Joanne had found herself spending more and more time writing at home. And even that did not protect her from regular interruptions.

"There was a phase when I had journalists at my front door quite a lot," she related to a *Newsweek* reporter. "And that was quite horrible. That was not something I had ever anticipated happening to me, and it's not pleasant."

But, like every other element of her newfound celebrity, Joanne had learned to deal with it. Which is why she took things like this just-concluded publicity trip in support of *Harry Potter and the Goblet of Fire* in stride. The town of Edinburgh was rounding into view. Joanne saw the familiar streets and buildings. In a short time, she would be taking Jessica in her arms and holding her tight.

Joanne Kathleen Rowling was the most famous author on the planet. But tonight she would just be Mom.

For the next couple of months, Joanne would once again return to normal pursuits. Every morning she would walk Jessica to school and pick her up at the end of the day. And she would find time to do some window shopping along Edinburgh's

Princess Street. She also did more interviews, a handful of appearances in bookstores in and around London and, to spare Jessica somewhat from the constant questions of classmates, Joanne did a pair of lectures as a reward for the two top performing classes in her daughter's school.

Joanne also began to turn her attention to charitable causes. She agreed to become the spokeswoman for the National Council for One Parent Families and donated $725,000 to the charity, whose emphasis was on helping single mothers. This was obviously a cause that was near and dear to Joanne's heart.

"I had a degree, a profession, and friends who were willing to lend me money when I badly needed it," she said in a speech before the organization. "So if I met obstacles pulling myself out of the benefits system, how much more difficult must it be for people who don't have the same advantages? Seven years after becoming a lone parent, I feel qualified to look anyone I meet in the eye and say that people bringing up children single-handedly deserve not condemnation, but congratulation."

Joanne's charitable outlook also led to her establishing a Harry Potter Fund with the charity group Comic Relief U.K., an organization dedicated to helping children in England and Africa.

Finally, when she had a few moments to herself, she secretly began writing the fifth Harry Potter book, *Harry Potter and the Order of the Phoenix.*

"I literally don't feel quite right if I haven't written for a while," she confessed during a *Newsweek* interview. "A week is about as long as I can go without getting extremely edgy. It really is a compulsion."

As summer began to turn to fall, Joanne realized that the quiet times were about to end and that she would soon be giving a reading before the largest audience she could ever imagine. The odyssey that would take her to Canada had begun almost a year earlier when she was racing to complete *Harry Potter and the Goblet of Fire.*

"I was feeling very fraught at the time," she told a Canadian Broadcast Corporation interviewer. "I was halfway through book four and I said yes. At that point, I did say yes to quite a lot of things just to stop people from asking me anything else because I really wanted to be writing. Then I sort of emerged from the madness that had been book four."

And realized exactly what she had said yes to.

As part of the festivities of the Vancouver International Writers' Festival, Joanne had agreed to do a pair of readings in the famed Pacific Coliseum in front of a projected sold-out audience of six thousand. But when word had leaked out that Joanne would be attending, the demand for tickets was so great that the festival directors had come back to Joanne with the request that she give an additional reading the day before in the Toronto Sky Dome, the home of the Toronto Blue Jays baseball team, in front of a projected twenty thousand young fans.

"I realized how big the reading was going to be and then I got terrified," she told the CBC interviewer.

Once she got over her initial fears, Joanne was thrilled at the prospect of going to Canada for the first time. The writer had always had a warm feeling about the country and its people and was looking forward to experiencing both "up close and personal" in what would be a six-day visit.

Joanne first flew into New York City, where she spent a couple of days meeting with her American publisher and giving a handful of magazine and newspaper interviews. Some of the questions covered familiar ground, but a few odd things had popped up in the wake of the publication of *Harry Potter and the Goblet of Fire* that she needed to address. One of the most outrageous to Joanne's many readers was the fact that, in the final sequence of the fourth book, there was a mistake in the order that Harry's parents emerge from Voldemort's wand. In the previous three books Joanne had said on several occasions that Voldemort had killed James first and Lily second. But in *Goblet of Fire* we are told that the ghosts would emerge in reverse order in which James steps out of the wand before Lily. Joanne exclaimed that it was just an unfortunate editing error that would be corrected in later editions of the book.

She was also questioned about why she was two months late in handing in the final manuscript of *Harry Potter and the Goblet of Fire*. She conceded that the book had been the hardest one to write and, while she had always taken great pains to be consistent in her story elements, that the plot basically got away from her.

"I wrote what I thought was half the book and suddenly realized that there was this huge, gaping hole in the middle of the plot," she explained to *Entertainment Weekly.* "The whole profile of the books got so much higher since the third book and there was an edge of external pressure."

Joanne explained that the problem arose when she had to pull a girl character, a Weasley cousin, because she had discovered that this character was serving the same function as investigative journalist, Rita Skeeter.

Joanne was sorry if the delays or other editorial errors confused her readers and assured them that more care would be taken with future books.

Joanne arrived in Toronto on October 22, 2000. Her first order of business would be something personal. She had been in contact with Valerie McDonald and had arranged to spend some time with the McDonald family and Annie Kidder on that first day. After arriving in Toronto, to no small amount of fanfare, and checking into her hotel, Joanne met with the McDonald family and Annie and spent what she would later state was a "wonderful" afternoon of sightseeing at Niagara Falls. But while this time with friends put her in an upbeat mood, the fear of doing a reading in front of an estimated 20,000 adoring fans once again was on her mind.

"I'm so terrified," she told the Knight Ridder News Service the day before the reading. "I'm not The Rolling Stones. How is this going to work?"

The day before the Sky Dome reading was taken up with a number of interviews and meeting representatives of her Canadian publisher. Joanne rather enjoyed meeting the press in Canada and patiently explained how her life had changed in the past few months since the publication of *Harry Potter and the Goblet of Fire*, retold some old stories about her early life that suddenly seemed fresh again, and dropped a few hints about the fifth Harry Potter book, already in progress.

During that busy day, Joanne also found the time to do some charitable works by appearing at a fund-raising luncheon for the Toronto Public Library. And despite signs stating that no autographs would be given during the luncheon, Joanne once again missed a meal when she willingly greeted and signed books for a steady stream of children who approached her.

But the main point of interest continued to be the Sky Dome reading scheduled for October 24. Ticket sales had been reportedly brisk for the event and an estimated twenty thousand fans would be in attendance. Joanne would acknowledge that she was delighted to be addressing so many of her fans at one time, but that there was still a lot of nervousness at the notion of reading Harry in the middle of a huge baseball field.

"I'm kind of looking at it like, if I can get through this, I can get through anything."

Joanne awoke the day of the reading with butterflies in her stomach. It was her big day.

The Sky Dome reading had been planned around a circus atmosphere. Children entering the stadium, many of whom were dressed as their favorite Harry Potter characters, were greeted by light shows and slide shows that projected elements of Harry Potter lore up on screens throughout the stadium as well as an indoor fireworks display. A group of outlandishly clothed wizards wandered through the stadium, performing magic tricks.

Prior to Joanne's appearance, a pair of Canadian children's authors, Tim Wynne Jones and Kenneth Oppel, read selections from their most recent books. But it was obvious that the young fans in the stands were far more interested in hearing Joanne.

Finally the event announcer stepped to the podium. Before he could even get out her name, the crowd erupted in a wave of applause and cheers. The moment had arrived. The stadium lights dimmed and Joanne moved to a podium in the center of the stadium and stood in the glare of a lone spotlight as the crowd went wild. The applause and cheers went on for some minutes as Joanne stood smiling and somewhat shocked at the response.

The thunderous applause continued as Joanne stepped up to the microphone.

"Thank you," she said, her voice echoing through the stadium. "I'm delighted and terrified to be here."

The crowd went silent.

Joanne took out her copy of *Harry Potter and the Goblet of Fire*, laid it on the podium, opened it to chapter four, and began to read. Almost immediately, her young fans, many of whom had brought their own copy of the new book, did likewise and began to read silently along with her.

Her stagefright now magically gone, Joanne, reading clearly and occasionally adding dramatic voices and accents, brought life to passages in her book in which the Dursleys are visited by an assortment of wizards. The children sat wide-eyed and enraptured. Many had tears streaming down their faces. For them, this was truly a magic time.

Fourteen minutes after she began reading, Joanne was finished. She closed her book as the cheers once again cascaded down around her. For the next fifteen minutes, she offered up answers to the most frequently asked questions about Harry Potter and his world. She finished by thanking the audience for coming and stepped off the stage to thunderous applause and the voice of the announcer urging the children to "read, read, read."

Joanne was deliriously happy as she stepped from the stage, receiving congratulations from friends and associates for a job well done. She was literally on a cloud the next two days as she journeyed to Vancouver, where she gave two more spirited readings before two sold-out audiences at Vancouver's famed Pacific Coliseum and, whenever possible, reached out to the children who would shyly approach her.

Prior to those readings, Joanne once again sat down with a group of reporters, and she stated her reason for agreeing to do a large reading like the one at the Sky Dome. She admitted that she would prefer the one-on-one contact that small readings and bookstore signings provided but that, sadly, those days appeared to be gone forever.

" 'If I did that now, I would never see my daughter," she said in a story that appeared on the Harry Potter fandom Web site. "I would never write another book. I would never eat or sleep. So I have to cut my cloth. I can say, 'Well, I won't read anymore,' which I would really miss. Or I could do bigger readings where I reach more people at once and that's the way I've chosen to go."

And while she told the assembled reporters that she considers book signings "a bottomless pit" that often test her mental and emotional strength, she willingly does them and for one big reason.

"I've never had a rude child, which for me is incredible. Never had one throw a tantrum. I've never had a child ask for more than I can give. Never once had a child for which I didn't feel anything but affection."

Joanne patiently answered the expected questions about dealing with success and what the future holds for Harry Potter. Although she would not like to admit it, Joanne was getting tired. And so she was grateful when the final round of applause greeted her last night in Vancouver.

Joanne knew it was time to go home.

She was missing her daughter terribly and, after six days of total adoration, was looking forward to returning to the simple life of writing at her favorite café, taking Jessica to and from school, and maybe doing a little shopping.

However, as her plane winged back across the Atlantic, she also knew that there would be something else awaiting her. Something that both excited and scared her.

The movie version of *Harry Potter and the Sorcerer's Stone* had begun filming two weeks earlier. And she could not begin to guess how a whole new world of Harry Potter would unfold.

11

IT'S ONLY A MOVIE

Joanne had flown to Los Angeles early in 2000 to finalize the contracts for the movie version of *Harry Potter and the Sorcerer's Stone.* And for Joanne, seeing the place where movie magic was made was an eye-opening experience. The negotiations were conducted in a cordial, straightforward manner in which Joanne's wishes were considered and honored.

Joanne had been cautious in dealing with the movie people. She had heard all too many stories about books being totally distorted in their transition to the screen and was fearful of the same thing happening to Harry. But in the end, Joanne came away from those meetings secure in the fact that the movie version of her book would be true to the world she created.

Joanne was given the title of executive producer when the deal was finalized with Warner Bros. to make the movie version of *Harry Potter and the Sorcerer's Stone*. Knowing little about how the movie business worked, she did not think much of the title at first. But as the various elements of the movie began to fall into place, she was glad she had it.

Because, as these things often happen in Hollywood, suggestions were soon being made that would change *Harry Potter and the Sorcerer's Stone* into something other than what the book had been. Early on Steven Spielberg had been considered the front-runner to direct the film. And Joanne had been thrilled with the idea of having the famed director of such films as *E.T.* and *Jurassic Park* create the Harry Potter world.

But during a series of meetings between Spielberg and Joanne, some very different opinions came to the surface. The director wanted to make a movie that would be more American, rather than English, in tone. There was talk of making many of the students and teachers international. But Joanne strenuously objected on the grounds that doing that would mean inventing characters that were not in the book. Spielberg went so far as to suggest that child actor Hayley Joel Osment, an American, would be the perfect choice to play Harry.

In the end, Joanne and the director respectfully agreed to disagree, and Spielberg moved on to another project. There was immediate speculation that Joanne and the famous director did not get along personally. But Joanne, ever the diplomat, said that it ultimately boiled down to a question of whose vision would ultimately wind up on the screen.

"There were things he said that I didn't agree with," she told the *London Times*. "There were things he said I did agree with."

There were also questions raised early on about the kind of merchandising tie-ins that would accompany the release of the film. That there would be fast-food restaurant toys, lunch boxes, dolls, and fully licensed Harry Potter action figures associated with the movie was a sensitive issue with

Joanne, who insisted that any merchandising connected with the film be tasteful and that a theme pushing literacy and reading be included. Warner Bros. was agreeable to much of what Joanne said—typified by the fact that Coca-Cola became an official sponsor of the film, but Harry would not be drinking a Coke in the film—and were in agreement that all associated items should be presented in a noncommercial manner.

Joanne insisted that, while she had basically sold the rights to let the studio do what they wanted, her opinion regarding the way Harry Potter was marketed had been taken into consideration by the studio. She had insisted, "Please trust me. I am fighting in your corner," when it came to how her creative "baby" was being sold.

"If the action figures are horrible, tell the kids I said don't buy them," she said in *Good Housekeeping*. The *New York Times* was also privy to the degree Joanne would defend her creation when she told them, "I would do anything to prevent Harry from turning up in fast-food boxes everywhere. I would do my utmost. That would be my worst nightmare."

A number of other directors were offered up to

Rowling before Chris Columbus was finally named early in 2000 to direct the film. Columbus and Joanne were on the same page when it came to how *Harry Potter and the Sorcerer's Stone* should be portrayed on the screen. They both agreed that the film should be, like the book, very British in tone and that it should be populated by largely British actors.

But when it was announced that American screenwriter Steve Kloves had been chosen to write the script for the movie, Joanne immediately had second thoughts.

"The person I was most nervous about meeting by far was Steve Kloves," she related in an *Entertainment Weekly* interview. "I was really ready to hate him. This was the man who was gonna butcher my baby. The first time I met him, he said, 'You know who my favorite character is?' And I thought, 'You're gonna say Ron.' But he said 'Hermione.' I just kind of melted."

Not too long after receiving the assignment to write the script, Kloves told *Reader's Digest* what he loved about Harry. "From the first page of book one, she had me. There's a genuine edge and darkness to it, and one reason she's so popular with children is that there's no pandering whatsoever."

He would recall in later months how the cordial relationship between Joanne and himself worked during the writing of the *Sorcerer's Stone* script. He explained that much of the dialogue in the script was his variation on what Joanne had written in her book. In doing that, Kloves felt he was anticipating some elements of the ongoing Harry Potter story that would come into play in later books.

"She reacted strongly," he reflected, in an Ain't It Cool Web site interview. "She was like, 'Ah, you sensed something but you also missed something.' In one instance, I put something in, a reference to something. She said, 'That's great but you can't do that because something's going to happen in book five that makes that impossible . . .'"

That Joanne would be such a stickler for details does not come as a surprise, because Harry Potter, in the ensuing years, had become much more than a fictional character. "I have known Harry and I have been writing about Harry for ten years," she explained to the *Los Angeles Times*. "He is very, very real to me."

The year 2000 found Joanne burning the candle at both ends, putting the finishing touches on *Harry Potter and the Goblet of Fire,* while monitoring the progress of Kloves's first draft of the script and sitting in on meetings on other aspects of the film-making process. With the director and writer in place, the next task was casting the film and, in particular, the all-important role of Harry Potter. The search for the perfect Harry was stretching worldwide with more than forty thousand child actors and just plain children auditioning for the role that would most certainly change their lives.

Joanne acknowledged that finding an actor to play Harry was proving difficult and that finding an actor with the right look and acting ability was a challenge equivalent to the search that led to the choice of actress Vivian Leigh to play Scarlett O'Hara in *Gone With The Wind.*

"We'll know him when we find him," she said to *Newsweek.* "I am now walking around in London and Edinburgh, and I'm looking at kids as I pass them, just thinking, Could be, you never know. I may just lunge at this kid and say, 'Can you act? You're coming with me. Taxi.' "

Initially, the movie studio had hoped to get

Harry Potter and the Sorcerer's Stone into theaters by summer 2001. But the combination of casting delays, lining up the incredible array of special effects and production design people necessary to bring the world of Harry Potter to the screen, and finding numerous London locations forced Warner Bros. to push back the release of the film to November 2001.

Casting the film was an ongoing challenge. Name actors as well as unknowns were being suggested for all roles. But midway through the year 2000, and a mere ten weeks before the start of filming, no actors had been cast.

Casting Harry continued to be the number one priority. More than eighty thousand letters went out soliciting actors to audition and the casting directors visited more than two hundred schools and numerous school drama departments. But the perfect Harry continued to be elusive.

Finally, on August 21, 2000, it was announced that eleven-year-old Daniel Radcliffe had been selected to play the coveted role of Harry Potter. The young British actor, who had previously appeared in the film biography of David Copperfield and the soon-to-be-released drama, *The Tailor of Panama,* was the spitting image of Harry Potter.

Joanne was ecstatic when she saw the youngster's screen test, feeling that after a long search, they had found their Harry. Director Chris Columbus was likewise thrilled.

"We saw so many enormously talented kids in the search for Harry," he said in an announcement on the Harry Potter Web site. "The process was intense, and there were times when we felt we would never find an individual who embodied the complex spirit and depth of Harry Potter. Then Dan walked into the room and we all knew that we had found Harry."

Radcliffe was officially presented as the film's Harry Potter in an August press conference. The youngster took easily to his new life in the spotlight as he patiently answered the media's questions.

"I cried and I was really excited," he said, in a *Hollywood Reporter* story. "I think I'm a tiny bit like Harry because I'd like to have an owl. I am looking forward to filming."

At the press conference, it was also announced that, since the movie would be titled *Harry Potter and the Sorcerer's Stone* in the United States and

Harry Potter and the Philosopher's Stone in the rest of the world, a total of seven scenes would be shot two different ways to allow for dialogue to include references to both titles.

Also cast as Harry's closest friends were ten-year-old Emma Watson as Hermione Granger and eleven-year-old Rupert Grint as Ron Weasley. With the core trio of roles now cast, the remainder of the all-important supporting characters quickly fell into place.

They were: Sean Biggerstaff (Oliver Wood), David Bradley (Argus Filch), John Cleese (Nick The Nearly Headless Ghost), Robbie Coltrane (Hagrid), Alfie Enoch (Dean Thomas), Tom Felton (Draco Malfoy), and Richard Griffiths (Uncle Dursley). Also cast were Richard Harris (Professor Dumbledore), Ian Hart (Professor Quirrell), Joshua Herdman (Gregory Goyle), Matt Lewis (Neville Longbottom), Rik Mayall (Peeves The Poltergeist), Devon Murray (Seamus), Katharine Nicholson (Pansy Parkinson) and Chris Rattling (Percy Weasley). Filling out the cast were Alan Rickman (Snape), Fiona Shaw (Aunt Petunia), Maggie Smith (Professor Minerva McGonagall), Verne Troyer (a ghoul), Zoe Wannamaker

(Madame Hooch), Julie Walters (Mrs. Weasley), and Jamie Waylett (Vincent Crabbe).

Harry Potter and the Sorcerer's Stone began filming in mid October 2000. It was cold in London as the cameras rolled for the first time. So cold that, when not shooting in the relative comfort of Leavesden Studios, heavy coats and hot water bottles were the order of the day.

As Joanne would find during her many visits to the set, her fears that Hollywood would do something bad to her story were unfounded. Under director Chris Columbus's direction, London locations as diverse as Christ Church College, the reptile section of the London Zoo, Oxford University, the famed Australia House and Durham Cathedral had been magically transformed into delightful, larger-than-life landmarks of the Harry Potter world.

Throughout the production, Joanne would constantly, by telephone, E-mail, and fax, be kept abreast of any last-minute script changes, casting additions, and the film's progress in general. She happily reported to *Entertainment Weekly,* "They [Warner Bros.] have been very gracious in allowing me input and I have been asked a lot of questions I never expected to be asked."

Typical of the attention to detail involved in the filming process was the day at King's Cross Station, where Harry boards The Hogwarts Express for his fateful trip to The Hogwarts School. A steam engine made to look like Joanne's fantastic creation sat idling on the track, awaiting Harry's leap of faith through the platform barriers. On either side of The Hogwarts Express were trains filled to overflowing with extras. Packed together on the platform were hundreds of child extras, many of them dressed in true-to-life Hogwarts uniforms, while others were wearing felt hats and cloaks. Scattered around the platform were luggage trolleys piled high with bags, trunks, and broomsticks.

Amid the clutter of cameras, cables, and crew people, director Columbus carried on an animated conversation with Daniel. There were smiles and laughs between them as Columbus instructed the actor on where to walk and how to look so he would be in the camera frame. Finally, the director called for action and the complex sequence of moving extras, trains, and all manner of technical challenges unfolded in one continuous take as Harry approaches the train and makes the life-changing decision to step aboard. The scene required a number of takes and the better part of a day to get right, but as the cast and crew wrapped up filming for the day, this important sequence was in the can.

Screenwriter Kloves, a frequent visitor to the *Sorcerer's Stone* set, came away with hints of other great moments. He claimed that sequences involving the flying broomsticks were "amazing" and that scenes featuring Hagrid looked "cool."

Reports would continue to filter out of the top-secret production—that the actors were doing an excellent job of bringing Joanne's creations to life and that the production designers and special effects people had made literal magic in bringing the Harry Potter universe to the screen. Joanne was heartened by the fact that her hopes for the film were finally being rewarded.

But the fantasy of filming *Harry Potter and the Sorcerer's Stone* occasionally ran afoul of reality. Much of the movie was being shot in the middle of England's often wet winter, and so the moviemakers would frequently have to shut down for the day because of rain. There were also some anxious moments when, because of his age and the laws regarding child actors, it was determined that, because of the delays, Daniel might not be able to finish the film. But after some careful negotiations, everybody had smiles on their faces and Daniel would be allowed to finish the movie.

The advance word on the film was so good that the movie studio announced that they had already approved the script for *Harry Potter and the Chamber of Secrets* and that filming of the second movie would begin before the end of 2001.

While *Harry Potter and the Sorcerer's Stone* would continue filming throughout the winter and into the summer months in London, Joanne was home in Edinburgh. Hard at work.

Joanne had never really had a timetable for completing any of her books in the early stages of her publishing career; instead, with few distractions, she had been able to complete the first books in the Harry Potter series in just about a year. But, as the worldwide popularity of the books developed and the demand for her time increased, Joanne was admittedly having a hard time conforming to her normal writing schedule. Plus, in the back of her mind, she felt that taking the extra time might help avoid the delays and errors that plagued *Harry Potter and the Goblet of Fire*.

And so while she had hoped to have the fifth

Harry Potter book out in time for the November 21, 2001, release of *Harry Potter and the Sorcerer's Stone,* midway through the year, Joanne would have to admit that she was not going to be able to complete the book. Her original goal had been to have Harry leaving Hogwarts as a full-fledged seventeen-year-old wizard in 2003. But now that goal has been put in doubt.

Because there would not be a Harry Potter book in 2001.

12

INTO THE FUTURE

Word quickly spread around the world that *Harry Potter and the Order of the Phoenix* would not be published until sometime in 2002.

Fans were disappointed and more than a little bit frustrated at the prospect of having to wait more than a year for their next Harry Potter adventure. So were Joanne's publishers, who had been hoping to make a big splash with the new Harry Potter book coming out at the same time as the movie version of *Harry Potter and the Sorcerer's*

Stone. And her publishers did put some pressure on her to try and meet the original timetable for the new book.

But Joanne stood her ground and refused to rush things.

"I really want to take my time and just make sure that it's as good as I can make it," she told a Knight Ridder News Service reporter. "I don't want to be running up against an artificial deadline. I'm working on it now and I have no intention of taking a break."

To those familiar with Joanne's writing habits and attention to detail, it did not come as too much of a surprise that *Harry Potter and the Order of the Phoenix* was lagging behind schedule. Despite the fact that Joanne had long ago plotted out the seven books of Harry Potter, she had always prided herself on her ability to restructure the story and play with elements of her characters to the point where she was finally satisfied. Consequently, it took a year or more to complete each of the first four Harry Potter books.

But according to close acquaintances, Joanne was suffering a bit of writer's fatigue based partly on the fact that she had, in hindsight, objected to the level of hysteria and secrecy surrounding the release of *Harry Potter and the Goblet of Fire.* In the aftermath of that experience, she was afraid that she would stop enjoying the writing process if she did not take a break and have a normal life.

So for a while, Joanne took things a little easier. She continued to write on a daily basis, but rather than pushing on when she became tired or distracted as she had in the past, she would stop writing. Joanne would often take leisurely walks through the city, or make time to be with her daughter and with family and friends. This less hectic approach to writing agreed with her, and Joanne would eagerly return to Harry each day with a new sense of excitement.

Now that it was common knowledge that Joanne was working on the fifth Harry Potter adventure, the curiosity began once again to grow. Jessica would often return from school and tell her mother that the children were pestering her with questions about what *Harry Potter and the Order of the Phoenix* was all about. And it was a favorite topic of conversation in the handful of interviews Joanne did during this period.

Not surprisingly, Joanne has refused to give

away too much information about the story line of book number five. But she has indicated that *Goblet of Fire* was the end of an era in Harry Potter's life and that *Harry Potter and the Order of the Phoenix* will point Harry's life in a totally different direction.

She hinted to the *New York Times* that Harry's "innocence is gone," that "the mood may darken," and that the death in book four is "the beginning of the deaths" that may continue in the next book. She also hints that in book five readers will discover why Harry returns to the Dursleys each summer and that Ginny Weasley, who had a crush on Harry in *Goblet of Fire,* will play a bigger role in the adventure. She also good-naturedly predicts that *Order of the Phoenix* will be scary, and that "Harry finds out a lot of things he hasn't stumbled across so far."

"Harry has already dealt with death," she told a Canadian Broadcast Corporation interviewer. "He lost his parents very young and in book four he witnessed a murder. So this is not news to anyone who has been following the series, that death is a central theme of the books. It would be fair to say that in book five he has to examine exactly what death means in closer ways. But I don't think people who have been following the series will be that surprised by that."

She also warned readers that book five will see Harry's horizons broadening, and that he will be entering totally new areas of his magical world.

But while *Harry Potter and the Order of the Phoenix* would not come out for a while, there would be some new Harry Potter–related books. Midway through 2000, Joanne came up with an idea to help fund one of her favorite charities, Comedy Relief U.K. She agreed to write two 64-page books, both under a pseudonym, based on titles that appear in the Hogwarts library, with all proceeds from sales going to Comedy Relief's Harry Potter Fund, which was formed with Joanne's cooperation to help fund children's causes.

The first book, *Quidditch Through the Ages,* is a fanciful, comprehensive guide to Quidditch and a resource guide to the magical world and its most popular sport. For this book, Joanne took the name Kennilworthy Whisp. The second book, *Fantastic Beasts and Where to Find Them,* is an A-to-Z listing of all the fantastic creatures that populate the world of Harry Potter. Joanne wrote this book under the name Newt Scamander.

"I have always wanted to write these two books," Joanne said in a press release announcing the books. "I thought it was a wonderful opportunity to be involved in a charity I have always supported."

Word quickly spread throughout Harry Potter fandom and the books were immediately snapped up upon their release in early 2001. Joanne would happily report that millions of dollars made from the sales of the two books had made their way into the Harry Potter Fund.

Joanne continued to use her writing for good works when she agreed to pen an original short story for a short-story collection—which will be published in 2002—that will raise money for the National Council for Single Parent Families. Little is known about Joanne's contribution except that Harry Potter would not be in it and that its story, in keeping with the theme of the book, would be about some element of magic.

As 2001 came to an end, Joanne would plan to enjoy the holidays close to home and with family and friends. Christmas would see Joanne and Jessica enjoying a huge dinner with her sister and her family; a highlight would be watching her brother-in-law, a chef, cook up the holiday turkey. New Year's would see Joanne and her daughter on holiday, taking in the sights and relaxing away from the constant demands on her time.

With her sister, Di, her family, and her close-knit circle of friends, Joanne could be assured of being treated as something other than a celebrity author. To these people, she was simply Joanne and that was fine with her. Because, in her heart, Joanne was basically a shy personality who was still coming to terms with the celebrity status that Harry Potter had brought her—to a large extent taking her away from the quiet life she had known. And while she now realized that she would forever be in the public eye, there was still a part of her that craved the privacy of a low-profile life.

After the first of the year, Joanne would return to the reclusive life of a writer, insulating herself from outside distractions as she continued to work on *Harry Potter and the Order of the Phoenix*. She was once again excited as the adventure continued, first in her mind and then on the page, at a steady pace. For Joanne, writing *Order of the Phoenix* was a welcome return to the quiet times she had experienced before her simple tales of Harry Potter had catapulted her into the spotlight.

But she could not completely hide from the notoriety that goes along with the fact that *Harry Potter and the Goblet of Fire* sold nearly 3 million copies in its first week and that there were nearly 50 million copies of her books in print in the United States alone. She has said that she has no idea if the worldwide mania for Harry Potter has reached its peak, and she is not sure if, even after four books, she has learned how to deal with the fame.

"I'm still learning," she told a group of reporters while in Canada. "I would definitely not say I'm on top of it. I would say that for the first two years of it, I was in denial. I kept thinking, 'It will go away.' And about the time of the publishing of the third book, I had to accept the fact that it wasn't going away any time soon, which is probably a healthier place to be. It will go away. That's the nature of the game. And when it does I believe I will be happy. And I will have fond memories of the time I was famous."

And the financial security that her fame has brought her. Joanne recently bought a second home in London, but anyone expecting her to spend her money frivolously on cars and helicopters, as was once speculated on in *Newsweek,* is sadly mistaken.

"Well, I can't drive so the five cars would be a problem," she laughingly explained in response to *Newsweek*'s question. "I don't want anyone thinking I'm a puritan. I enjoy spending money. But the main difference between where I was five years ago and now is the absence of worry. I honestly believe that the only people who will really appreciate that are people who have been very, very broke. What I'm grateful for every day is that I'm not worried about the money."

Money has always been a rather sticky subject with Joanne. It has been speculated often in newspapers and magazines about how much Joanne has made and how rich she is. Joanne has often refused to put an actual number to her riches. But she did recently state in a *Philadelphia Inquirer* interview that "I could not write anymore and never have to worry about not having money again."

Joanne's notoriety and generous contributions to local charities have done much to make the author an unofficial ambassador for England and a favorite of the Royal Family. Early in the year 2001, Joanne was invited to their Gloucestershire country home for a meeting with Prince William, in which the heir to the throne complimented her on her books and her devotion to charity. On March 22, she was delighted and quite humbled when she had an audience with Queen Elizabeth on the occasion of a meeting between the Queen and members of the British publishing industry.

It was also during this time that Joanne fell in love.

Not much was known about how the couple met or who the man was, but what was known was that whenever spotted walking hand-in-hand on the streets of Edinburgh, they seemed deliriously happy. Personally and professionally, Joanne appeared to be in a state of grace.

In terms of her chosen profession, she also considered herself very lucky.

"It [writing] has made me happier," she said in a *Newsweek* interview. "Finishing them [the books] has made me happier. It also makes me happy that the one thing I thought I could do, I wasn't deluded."

And she was now looking to the future.

Uppermost in her mind was the future of the remaining books in the Harry Potter odyssey. Speculation is that book six will be titled *Harry Potter and the Green Flame Torch,* a rumor Joanne would deny. What she would speculate on was that she sees the remaining books as an exploration of the many personal and magical elements of Harry's character as he moves through his teen years. She sees the possibility of a romantic relationship for Harry and a more realistic interaction with the world around him. And while the final adventure of Harry Potter is still a few years off, Joanne is already looking forward to that finale.

"Book seven will be the biggest," she predicted in a *Newsweek* interview. "Seven is going to be like the *Encyclopaedia Britannica* because I'm going to want to say good-bye."

How she ultimately chooses to end the odyssey of Harry is still a mystery. Although she has acknowledged that she has already written the last chapter to the last book, doing so was mostly an act of faith to show that she really will get there in the end. Joanne is not quite sure what leads up to that moment. "Besides I might just end up rewriting that chapter," she joked during an online chat.

But, she offered the *Philadelphia Inquirer*, certain emotional elements of the final Harry Potter book are already in place. "By the series end you feel a sense of resolution. You find out what happens to the survivors, to those characters who live through all seven books. I know that sounds very ominous."

In the coming months, Joanne will remain the authority on her world as she oversees the completion of the movie version of *Harry Potter and the Sorcerer's Stone* and checks her E-mail regularly for missives from screenwriter Steven Kloves, who is already hard at work on the script for *Harry Potter and the Chamber of Secrets*. In fact, Warner Bros. has recently finalized a deal for the film rights to all seven Harry Potter books, which means that long after Joanne has written the literal last word on Harry, her legacy will be on the screen well into the next decade.

But with the self-imposed end of Harry Potter now in sight, Joanne looks at her creation with mixed emotions. "I think when I've finished the seven Harry Potter books, I will be finished with the world," she ventured in a Barnes & Noble online chat. "It will make me very sad to say good-bye, but it must be done."

Of course there were the rumors. The world-wide success of the Harry Potter books had been so massive that, reportedly, Joanne's publishers were hinting that it would be great if Joanne took Harry out of Hogwarts and into the world as a full-fledged wizard. Although Joanne would publicly laugh off the notion of carrying Harry's adventures further than the projected seven books, she would occasionally tantalize a reporter with the notion that yes, indeed, there were still stories that could be told.

"I always said there would be seven," she said in an America Online chat. "If there's ever an eighth, it will be because, ten years down the line, I had a burning desire to do just one more. But I don't presently think that will happen. However, I think I might write a kind of 'Harry Potter Encyclope-dia' and give the royalties to charity."

And she indicated in the same chat that the notion of continuing to write children's books was also a possibility. "I might write more children's books. I really don't know. I should say, however, that I do not feel I have to write my 'serious' adult book to be a 'proper' author. The idea comes first, not the target audience."

Harry Potter and the Sorcerer's Stone was scheduled to complete filming in the summer of 2001. Joanne, during her periodic visits to the filming, had been impressed and amazed at how her world was being translated from the page to the screen. The excitement continued into the fall as the publicity machine for the film switched into high gear. Everywhere she turned, she saw Harry or selected images from the film. The film studio was being cautious not to overpublicize the movie, but the early reaction to the bits and pieces of the film that were made available in movie theaters and on television created an excitement around the coming movie that easily rivaled the arrival of each new Harry Potter book. As the days counted down to the November release of the film, Joanne could not help but find herself anticipating the movie, right along with her fans.

It was a good feeling.

"I'm going to be sitting there like everybody else, really wanting to watch Quidditch," she told

CNN interviewer Larry King. "That's the thing I want to see most. I've been watching this inside my head for ten years so to be able to physically watch it on the screen. I feel like a kid when I think about it."

13

REAL LIFE . . .
FANTASY LIFE

That childlike feeling remained with Joanne through the days and weeks leading up to the November 2001 release of *Harry Potter and the Sorcerer's Stone*. Finally, in October 2001, Joanne was told that the film was completed and a special screening was scheduled for her. On the appointed day, she entered a screening room, settled into her seat, and waited for the lights to go down.

Any concerns she had about how her literary child would be treated by Hollywood soon dissolved as she watched the images flicker across the screen. A smile appeared on her face that would not fade for days. Inside there was a sigh of relief.

Hollywood had gotten Harry Potter right.

"I'd say a week from seeing the film I was very excited," she reported to a CBBC *Newsround* interviewer. "And the closer the viewing came, the more frightened I became. When I actually sat down to see the film, I was terrified; because it was way too late if any of the bits were wrong. But at the end of the film I was happy. There's an awful lot of my book up there. All the important bits, I'd say."

She would later state that she was particularly pleased with the way the actors had brought her characters to life and quite amazed at the way modern filmmaking and the wizardry of special effects had succeeded in making her most imaginative notions a big screen reality.

When *Harry Potter and the Sorcerer's Stone* finally opened in November to rave reviews, Joanne was barely paying attention to the critical success the movie of her beloved book had become. This was because she was hard at work on the latest installment of the Harry Potter series, *Harry Potter and the Order of the Phoenix*, and was already hearing anxious inquiries about when the next book would be completed.

Joanne is not the kind of writer to be rushed, but she realized that with the first four Harry Potter books being delivered on an almost yearly basis, her loyal fans had come to expect new Harry Potter adventures on a regular and timely schedule and that she had, in a sense, spoiled them. But her feelings were that it would be giving less than her best effort to rush something out before she was satisfied that it was her best effort.

And besides, at the moment there was something that was equally, if not more important to Joanne.

She was in love and she was preparing to be married.

For years Joanne felt that with her struggles to make a life for herself and her daughter, Jessica, and her attempts to make a living as a writer, there was little time for love and romance in her life. And truth be known, while she had a beautiful daughter to show for her first marriage, the unhappy way it had ended was making her a bit shy about once again attempting a relationship and possibly falling in love. But, by 1998, with Harry Potter a worldwide success, Joanne told the *Sunday Telegraph,* "I have what I always wanted. Now let's get Mr. Perfect in."

Joanne was introduced to Dr. Neil Murray, an anesthesiologist, in the early part of 2001 at a party given by a mutual friend of both. She was immediately attracted to his boyish good looks, sly sense of humor, and the fact that he was not awestruck by her notoriety. It also did not hurt that, with his slightly tousled dark hair, fully angular face, and glasses, he bore a striking resemblance to her creation, Harry Potter, as a grown-up. Was that part of the attraction? Only Joanne knows for sure. And she's not telling.

"The night we met, he told me he had read the first ten pages of *Philosopher's Stone* and he thought it was quite good," Joanne recalled in a recent London *Times* interview. "And I thought that was fantastic. He hadn't read the books. He didn't really have a clear idea of who I was. It meant that we could get to know each other in a quite natural way."

Joanne and Neil hit it off immediately and began dating right away. Getting to know Neil was easy. He was a good talker and a good listener. He had interests and a job that, like Joanne, he was passionate about. With Neil, Joanne could talk about anything or nothing and feel at ease. For Joanne, dating was an experience she had almost forgotten, but in the ensuing months their casual relationship, as they walked the streets of Edinburgh and dined at little bistros and pizzerias, turned quickly into love.

Neil and Jessica got along famously, which, for Joanne, was the primary consideration in any personal relationship. And Neil's easygoing nature was not threatened by the compromises that had to be made in their private time, when Joanne had to write or deal with some other chores connected to her creation, Harry Potter. It did not bother him when they were out and about and Joanne would be approached for an autograph or by an anxious child who wanted to talk to her about Harry. The young doctor's lack of ego and security made him even more attractive to Joanne.

Like everything else in her life, Joanne was adamant about keeping her relationship with Neil away from the public and the prying eyes of the press. But it was not long before the newspapers got wind of the man in Joanne's life and their relationship and their names became regularly linked in gossip columns around the world. Joanne was frustrated at the intrusion, but knew it could not be helped, and so she and Neil adopted a humorous attitude toward their private life going public.

By July 2001, Joanne and Neil were head over heels in love and ready to be married. Knowing that any public ceremony would bring the press out by the hundreds and would destroy any sense of the quiet, private ceremony the couple wanted, Joanne and Neil decided that, during a secret, romantic cruise to the Galápagos Islands, they would sneak away and be married in secret. Plans were made and those few people who they wanted present at their wedding were notified.

Unfortunately the press found out about their plans, and the normally sedate Galápagos Islands were soon swarming with reporters and photographers. They placed inquiring calls to Neil's parents and to Joanne's publisher and agent. Joanne and Neil, feeling that their quiet wedding was about to turn into a three-ring media circus, called off the wedding plans.

For the moment.

As the months played out, Joanne and Neil fell

deeper in love. She was on his arm at the premiere of *Harry Potter and the Sorcerer's Stone* in November, and it was at that time that the couple purchased the mansion in the town of Abferdly and made plans to make it their permanent residence once they were officially husband and wife. Their public appearances together and the growing knowledge by the world that Joanne and Neil were a couple made their desire to be joined together in the eyes of God in marriage become even stronger. Finally, as a Christmas present to themselves, Joanne and Neil decided to get married on December 26, 2001. And this time they were determined to avoid the prying eyes of the press.

To avoid any leaks, the couple asked a minister from outside the area they lived in to perform the ceremony. They went fifty miles outside of Edinburgh to hire the caterers for the reception that would follow the ceremony. A short list of fifteen family, friends, and relatives who would attend the ceremony were sworn to secrecy. And rather than a big church in the center of Edinburgh for the ceremony, the happy couple chose to say their vows in the hallowed halls of Killiechassie House, a mansion tucked in the out-of-the-way town of Aberfeldy.

On December 26, Joanne Kathleen Rowling and Neil Murray were united in marriage in a twenty-minute ceremony inside the cavernous halls of Killiechassie House. Joanne's daughter, Jessica, served as one bridesmaid. Her sister, Dianne, and Neil's sister, Lorna, were also bridesmaids. Joanne, radiant in a cream-colored wedding gown, had seen a big part of her fantasy life become a reality.

However, the fantasy of that most perfect day would be short-lived, as reality once more entered their lives. Joanne was starting to feel the pressure to finish the latest Harry Potter adventure and conceded that she would not feel comfortable taking an extended honeymoon with that specter hanging over them. And so the couple agreed that they would postpone their honeymoon until Joanne had completed *Harry Potter and the Order of the Phoenix*.

Following the wedding, Neil returned to his anesthesiology practice while Joanne plunged eagerly into the task at hand, completing the book that the whole world was anxiously waiting for. There was a renewed sense of excitement and joy as the pages began to pile high. Joanne would occasionally drop little hints of what was to come in this latest installment of the Harry Potter odyssey. The fifth book would be approximately eight hundred pages long and would contain thirty-eight chapters. There was the notion that as characters grew into their teen years, the tone of their relationships would change, and there was the persistent statement that at least one of the ongoing characters from the first four books would not survive to book six.

"It's dark," Joanne would hint at during a 2002 BBC interview. "There's a really bad death in it that I have not enjoyed writing."

Joanne continued to tantalize readers during the press interviews as she dropped further, often more detailed hints about what was to come in *Harry Potter and the Order of the Phoenix.*

In one interview she stated, "The Dursleys are in the next book and there's stuff coming with them that people might not expect." In another she reported, "Harry will see the real Mad Eye Moody in book five." In yet another, she said, "Why do some wizards become ghosts and the others don't? You will find out much more about that in book five."

Rowling seemed to enjoy dropping hints to her

curious fans about what the future of Harry Potter would bring. In one interview, she hinted that the key to what would happen in the last three books could be found in *Harry Potter and the Goblet of Fire* when Dumbledore tells his students that they have to make a choice between what is right and what is easy. "This is the setup for the next three books," said Joanne. "All of the characters are going to have to choose because what is easy is often not right."

When a fan innocently asked the author what she would do if she were in Hogwarts for an hour, Joanne replied, "I would go straight into a certain room mentioned in book four which has certain magical properties Harry hasn't discovered yet."

Finally, as an aside to her characters, who were now deep in their teen years, Joanne said "They are fifteen now and their hormones are working overtime. Something is going to go on between Ron and Hermione but Ron doesn't realize it yet. Typical boy."

But the tidbits would only put fans off for so long and, as the weeks and months went by and the new book was nowhere near completion, the rumors began to circulate on a worldwide basis that

Joanne had suddenly developed writer's block and was having trouble completing the book. Some had even suggested that married bliss with Neil was taking Joanne away from the task at hand. The British book publisher, Bloomsbury, the American publisher, Scholastic, and Warner Bros., the company producing the Harry Potter movies, had hoped for the perfect tie-in, the movie version of *Harry Potter and the Chamber of Secrets* and *Harry Potter and the Order of the Phoenix* coming out on the exact same day in November 2002.

However, by May, with no manuscript completed and the rumors and fan reaction turning to frustration, a public response was needed. Rebecca Salt, a spokesperson for Joanne, issued a short but concise statement that month that "rejected any suggestion that Rowling was suffering from writer's block."

That did little to placate the fans, who had by now calculated that it had been two and a half years since the last Harry Potter adventure. Joanne was giving few interviews at this point, preferring to concentrate on completing the new Harry Potter book. In a rare conversation with *Newsround* midway through 2002, she addressed the issue of the seemingly tardy book.

"There's a lot of the book done," she said. "That's all I want to say because if I give a date and then I pass it, everyone will be upset. I will say that I have a beginning, a middle, and an end. You could read it all the way through and I know a lot of Harry Potter fans will say, 'Just give it to us.' But I'm a perfectionist and I want more time to tweak it. I have to laugh when I read bits about writer's block because I don't think I've ever been blocked in my life."

Unfortunately such public statements did little to slow down the press. When there was no further news coming directly from Joanne, reporters began turning up in the town of Aberfeldy, asking people on the street, in cafés, and other places of business if Joanne had been out and about and if they knew anything about her progress on the fifth book. The people were not talking. After the initial curiosity of having a world-famous author living in their town, the townsfolk had warmed to Joanne and her family and their down-to-earth ways and had become very protective of her privacy. So while the people of Aberfeldy knew nothing about Joanne and her writing life, even if they did they would not say.

One secret that would be revealed in the following months was that, while reportedly writing *Harry Potter and the Order of the Phoenix,* Joanne was taking some time off to tackle another writing project, one she would later describe as "a novel," possibly "adult in nature" and something that, to this date, remains unfinished.

Joanne continued to use her popularity to do a number of personal and charitable good works. In April 2002, it was reported that Joanne had turned over the deed to her old house in Edinburgh, Scotland, to a longtime friend, Fiona Wilson. Wilson, also a single mother, had been a supporter and confidante of Joanne's during her struggling days.

Long a supporter of single parent rights and funding, Joanne's voice was often raised in protest against the government's plans to cut funding for single parent services. She would make the point that single mothers trying to get by on government support were often in a degrading situation. Joanne pointed out that the depiction of her life as a single mother in her pre–Harry Potter days was part and parcel of the problem of dealing with the needs of single mothers.

"Some articles written about me have come close to romanticizing the time I spent on Income Support," she told *The Daily Mirror.* "The well-worn cliché of the writer starving in a garret is so much more picturesque than the bitter reality of living in poverty with a child. The reality was that I was humiliated by poverty."

The writer also continued to be a strong and outspoken supporter of the plight of multiple sclerosis patients. The sad memories of her mother's passing from the disease were still a harsh memory in her mind that would bring her sadness almost daily.

Joanne did more than talk about the problem of single parent families. With the cooperation of the British charitable organization The National Council of One Parent Families, Joanne was instrumental in putting together a fundraising short story collection, entitled *Magic,* to raise money for the organization. The book features stories by such notable British authors as Sue Townsend, Fay Weldon, Jo Harris, Arabella Weir, Meera Syal, Ben Okri, and Christopher Brookmyre. Originally

Joanne had thought about writing an original short story for the collection. Eventually she changed her mind and, instead, decided to write a foreword to the collection that chronicles in harsh detail, the often humiliating and degrading lifestyle she had led as a struggling single mother. *Magic* would ultimately earn more than $1 million for the charity.

While Joanne remained front and center and very public in such high-profile causes, a sense of privacy would always enter into those other small but no less noble causes that would, inevitably, involve children who were sick or dying. And, because of her private nature, her good deeds would often not reveal themselves until weeks, months, or years after the fact.

When a nine-year-old child named Abbey Cape had survived a near-death experience and a life-saving heart transplant earlier in the year, Joanne, upon hearing of the young girl's plight, sent her a toy owl and a note of encouragement.

Easily the most heart-wrenching encounter Joanne ever had involved the plight of six-year-old Albany, New York, native Catie Hoch. Catie, a loyal Harry Potter fan, had been diagnosed with a severe form of childhood cancer. Catie and her mother, Gina, were near the end of reading *Harry Potter and the Prisoner of Azkaban* when the doctors revealed that the cancer was spreading and that young Catie only had weeks to live.

Catie, like all Harry Potter readers, was desperate to find out what happened next, and her mother felt that any kind of contact with her favorite author would help ease her last days. A family friend sent an e-mail to Joanne's publisher explaining Catie's story and asking if it would be possible for Joanne to get in touch with the dying child. Joanne was touched and deeply saddened and immediately sent off a personally written letter that she signed simply "Jo."

This began an e-mail correspondence in which Joanne enthralled the sick child with bits and pieces of information on the latest book, *Harry Potter and the Goblet of Fire,* which she was working on at the time. Sadly, Catie's illness continued to progress and, at one point, it was determined that Catie only had days to live. Joanne made a fateful decision and arranged to call Catie personally and read whole segments of the yet-to-be-published *Harry Potter and the Goblet of Fire* over the telephone.

Catie's mother Gina told the *Sunday Mirror,* "We laid Catie down on the couch and Jo read to her over the phone. Catie's face lit up. I will be forever grateful for what Jo gave us. She gave us something priceless by having this relationship with Catie."

Joanne called Catie and read to her on four separate occasions. Sadly, the child's condition worsened and Catie died on May 18, 2000. Following her death, Joanne told Catie's parents that their little girl had left "footprints on my heart."

Throughout the months of 2002, Joanne, Neil, and Jessica had settled into a rather quiet routine. Jessica, precocious but wise beyond her years, was off to school. As she grew older, Jessica had learned to deal with having a celebrity mother and had turned out to be quite a levelheaded, normal child. Neil was working steadily at St. Johns Hospital in nearby Livingston. Joanne occasionally did some window shopping in Aberfeldy and the family took the odd couple of days for a holiday, but, for the most part, Joanne was hard at work on *Harry Potter and the Order of the Phoenix.*

Unfortunately the notoriety surrounding her early writing habits made it impossible for her to go to a coffee shop, sit at a table, and write. But she had adjusted nicely to the well-ordered writing room in her new home. However, she would admit in an interview with the Broughton High School magazine, *The High,* that she did indeed miss those quiet days of writing by hand at a table at The Nicholson Café with her then-baby Jessica sleeping soundly at her feet.

"I still see a large café with a window seat as my ideal writing place," she said. "A large café with a small corner table overlooking an interesting street that would serve strong coffee and be nonsmoking."

Work on the new book was proceeding at a steady pace. Joanne was encouraged by her progress; so much so that, during a midyear interview with the *Times,* she answered "probably" when asked about the possibility of the new book being out for Christmas. "The manuscript is stacked nice, neat, pristine, and big," she added.

But the perfectionist in Joanne knew that the reality was that it would be a while longer until she had *Harry Potter and the Order of the Phoenix* at the point that she felt she had done all the tweaking and fixing she could do.

During this time, Joanne was being kept abreast of the film of the second Harry Potter adventure, *Harry Potter and the Chamber of Secrets*. Director Chris Columbus and screenwriter Steve Kloves were set to repeat their roles on *Chamber of Secrets*, and it gave Joanne much comfort that these experienced hands would once again be involved in interpreting her work. She felt the script for the second film was truly faithful to the book. She was also happy that, as in the first film, actors would come to her with any questions they had about how to play their characters. Joanne would receive progress reports from the set and was heartened by the continued use of traditional structures and locations in and around London and Scotland for the film.

Harry Potter and the Chamber of Secrets started filming three days after the first Harry Potter movie had opened in theaters. Director Chris Columbus stated that he knew that *Chamber of Secrets* would be a different kind of film.

"There are similar elements (to both films) but this one is a little darker, a little edgier, and a lot more exciting," Columbus told the BBC. "One of the things we benefited from the second time around was that we'd set up the characters in the first film so we could immediately get into the story."

The director also acknowledged that a big plus in the second film was that the main child actors were more confident and comfortable in their roles. "They'd been doing it for a hundred fifty days on the first film and so they came to *Chamber of Secrets* with a newfound confidence so their performances were better."

Like everyone else, there was a lot of curiosity on Joanne's part as she monitored the progress of the film.

The film's three child actors, Daniel Radcliffe, Emma Watson, and Rupert Grint, were now a year older but so, she reasoned, were the characters in the book. The darker nature of *Chamber of Secrets* was cause for momentary concern, but Joanne quickly realized that the children who had read her books should have no problem accepting the fantastic and often nightmarish images on screen.

Joanne reflected on her lack of concern with how the movies would treat her books during an interview conducted with reporters from the Broughton High School magazine, *The High,* shortly after the release of the movie version of *Harry Potter and the Chamber of Secrets.*

"I was originally nervous about letting my books be made into films because I did not feel I was far enough into the series. I didn't want non-author-written sequels where a film company could have taken my characters and send them off to Las Vegas on holiday or something equally mad. I finally said yes when I knew I was far enough into the books to make it difficult for the filmmakers to take Harry and company in directions I didn't want them to go."

It was at the point where the media attention for the movie was at its highest that the rumor surfaced that Joanne had secretly taken time off from writing and traveled to a well-hidden movie location, where she reportedly filmed a small cameo role for the movie. Joanne laughed when she heard it. It would be fun to do. But at that time she had neither the desire nor the time to play movie actor.

Joanne continued to work on *Harry Potter and the Order of the Phoenix* throughout the winter and well into the summer months. The happiness of her married life was a constant boost to her spirits. Jessica had become the bright, intelligent young girl Joanne had hoped and prayed she would be. Neil, a hardworking, dedicated, and loving man, was always there for her in every way. But Joanne would have those days when even the warmth of family and home were not enough to put a smile on her face.

The pressure and expectation generated around the world for the coming Harry Potter book was hard to hide from. It was a pressure that became even more a part of her life when she realized that, despite her best efforts, she was not going to be able to finish the book for a December 2002 publication, for which she had hoped.

Adding to the stress were various new elements of the characters in the new book, especially Harry. Everyone's favorite wizard, Joanne would later report, was dealing with a lot of anger in this book and the first hints of teenage romance, which were challenging elements for Joanne. Also, Joanne had decided that she was going to kill off a recognizable character in *Order of the Phoenix,* a daring step in any case but one that is always a major risk in children's books. The stress of the death finally reached the breaking point one day when Neil found Joanne in the kitchen, sobbing uncontrollably.

"I had rewritten the death, rewritten it, and that was it," Joanne said in a story in *The Australian*. "The person was definitely dead."

Ever the supportive spouse, Neil suggested that if it was making her this upset, perhaps she should not kill the character. Joanne told him, "Well, it just doesn't work like that. When you're writing a children's book, you need to be a ruthless killer."

While writing, Joanne was also reflective of the good and bad sides of fame that her creation had brought her. The good side was that she would never have a material need again, which meant lifelong security for her and her family. The down side was that her life as a successful author had put her permanently in the public eye and Joanne, who continued to be a shy and private person after years of being in a literal fishbowl, was not always happy with the idea of standing out from the crowd or the constant demands made on her free time. Neil and Jessica were completely understanding of those demands and didn't complain.

Joanne continued to be frustrated at what she felt was an unnecessary intrusion on her family time and writing time and she told a reporter for *Scotsman.com* about that frustration. "There were times when I would gladly give back some of the money in exchange for the time and peace to write. That's been the biggest strain. I've become famous and I'm not very comfortable with that. Because of the fame, some really difficult things have happened and it's required a great effort of will to shut them out. There have been some black weeks when I've wondered whether it's worth it but I've plowed on."

Unfortunately the task at hand seemed to become more difficult midway through the summer. Joanne was having a hard time focusing on the work and she was beginning to feel strangely out of sorts. A trip to the doctor confirmed what she surely suspected.

Joanne was pregnant.

14

SECRETS REVEALED . . . LIFE GOES ON

Joanne was caught up in a swirl of emotions at the news. But one thing was certain. . . .

The tears that ran down her cheeks were tears of happiness.

Neil was thrilled at the news that he was going to become a father for the first time. Jessica was excited at the prospect of having a younger brother or sister in the house. Once the initial rush of excitement died down, Joanne turned practical in the face of this blessed event. She reasoned that announcing her pregnancy to the world this soon would only add to the pressure already on her because of the coming Harry Potter book, which by July 2002 was still not completed, and the buzz on the second Harry Potter movie, which was already being speculated on by the media as being so dark and scary that it might frighten much of the Harry Potter audience. With all of this going on, she decided, quite logically, to hold off on an initial announcement of her pregnancy for a couple of months.

Joanne wrote at a consistent pace throughout the remainder of the summer as she fine-tuned and added creative flourishes to a manuscript that would ultimately total more than 250,000 words. Joanne's thoughts, however, were never far from the baby slowly growing inside her stomach. She daydreamed about the future and the joy and happiness that this new child would bring to their lives.

By September, rumors were already beginning to spread that the author of the Harry Potter books was, indeed, with child, and so she felt the time was right to make an official announcement. And so a spokesperson for Joanne, Nicky Stonehill, released a simple statement that said: "J. K. Rowling and Dr. Neil Murray are expecting a baby in the spring."

The response to the news was totally positive. The Internet chatrooms were abuzz with questions of whether it would be a boy or a girl or what its name would be. It was around this time that one of the many rumors that always seemed to be circulating around Joanne and Harry Potter surfaced.

It was reported by a number of press sources that titles for the sixth, seventh, and, yes, an eighth Harry Potter book had already been selected; the titles allegedly being *Harry Potter and the Pyramids of Furmat, Harry Potter and the Chairiots of Light,* and *Harry Potter and the Alchemist's Cell.* More amused than angry, Joanne told a BBC reporter "No one, literally no one, not in my family or anybody else, knows the titles to books six and seven and I'm going to keep it that way for now."

Regarding a reported book eight, Joanne declared that she had no plans for Harry beyond book seven and, if she did do an additional Potter book, it would most likely be an encyclopedia of the Harry Potter world whose proceeds would go to charity.

Joanne had settled into a comfortable routine as she continued to polish *Harry Potter and the Order of the Phoenix.* When not writing she would often find herself staring out the windows of her

home into the quiet of the surrounding countryside and woods and reflecting on a number of
things: the coming baby, her happy marriage to a
wonderful man, and the sheer wonderment of
watching Jessica as she grew. She was a lucky
woman. She was also a woman who continued to
find ways of helping others.

As Halloween grew close, Joanne had braced
herself for the endless parade of Harry Potter characters tramping through towns and cities all over
the world in search of treats. She felt it a compli-
ment but also thought that something should be
done during the holiday season to help others.

Joanne had an idea . . . to make Hogwarts a
reality.

After a series of telephone calls, Joanne discovered that historic Stirling Castle in Scotland was
available for functions. Under her expert guidance,
Stirling Castle, with its hallowed halls and ancient
pathways and ballrooms, was magically transformed into her fantasy institution, Hogwarts. Special invitations were sent out. For the sum of 250
pounds, one could spend a night in Hogwarts,
with the money to be donated to a charity repre-
senting multiple sclerosis. And so on the night of

November 1, 2002, invited guests were regaled by characters straight out of Harry Potter wandering the castle. Assorted wizards and magicians plied their trade. A sumptuous dinner was held and an auction of Hogwarts-related items was held. All in all, it was a grand night for a good cause in which an estimated 275,000 pounds was raised.

The next day was an important one for Joanne. She was excitedly primping and preparing herself for the London premiere of *Harry Potter and the Chamber of Secrets*. Just as for the previous film, Joanne was again a flutter with a mixture of excitement, nervousness, and curiosity. For her the same questions needed to be answered all over again.

That night, Joanne, on the arm of Neil and, by now, five months pregnant, was radiant as she walked down the red carpet at the Odeon Leicester Theater, through an unexpected rainstorm, smiling nervously as the expected press photographers' cameras clicked away in a constant explosion of flashbulbs. But as she bravely stood, allowing the press their photos, a smiling and supportive Neil at her side, she looked past the photographers . . . and was amazed.

Lines of fans, wearing outrageous costumes and

all done up in Hogwarts colors, had shown up at the premiere, with no hope of getting in the theater. She waved enthusiastically to them before entering the theater.

People magazine reported that Joanne, that night, was heard to remark, "I didn't think it would ever be this mad. When I wrote the book it would have been insane for me to imagine all this."

Once again she was hopeful as the lights dimmed. Once again she was rewarded. Chris Columbus and Steven Kloves had worked their magic, and Harry and his world came alive on the screen. The characters had continued to grow and mature. The scary bits were scary enough but not too scary. Hollywood had captured the magic of her books and her fertile imagination.

In fact, Joanne was so happy with the film that she overcame her shyness and willingly stopped to talk with the media after the screening. And it was at that point that a BBC reporter managed to get the information that the entire world had been waiting so long to hear.

"I'm putting the finishing touches on the manuscript," she said. "I'm weeks away from delivering it to the publisher. I'm really pleased with it. I'm just going to tweak it a tiny bit more and then the publishers will have it."

True to her word, the completed manuscript for *Harry Potter and the Order of the Phoenix* was turned over to Bloomsbury during the first days of December 2002.

Encouraging children to read continued to be one of Joanne's main cultural crusades, and she used that cause as an excuse to tantalize her fans with snippets of what was to come with her latest book. Joanne penned a ninety-three-word document in which she revealed some of the plot of *Harry Potter and the Order of the Phoenix*. She turned the document over to the famed London auction house Sotheby's to be auctioned off on December 12, with all proceeds going to Book Aid International. Word quickly spread about this highly collectible item, and the bidding was spirited on the day of the auction. When the gavel finally came down, the document had been sold for $45,300 to an American collector whose identity was kept secret.

With *The Order of the Phoenix* behind her, Joanne suddenly had quite a bit of free time. Much of it was devoted to Jessica and preparing for the arrival of her second child. Joanne could also often be found in the Harry Potter Internet chatrooms, under a false name, sending and receiving thoughts and impressions of the Harry Potter universe with children. Joanne had become familiar with the Internet while writing her second book, *Harry Potter and the Chamber of Secrets,* and became fascinated with the notion of communicating through cyberspace.

"Typing your thoughts into the ether and getting answers back, you don't know who is answering you."

Joanne was also using this time to get off by herself for a few hours, usually to go into Edinburgh for a bit of shopping or to do some errands. It was during these moments that she would often dress rather informally and very unlike the image that had grown up around her as a prim and proper writer. Joanne would usually go unnoticed during these trips but, according to a *People* magazine article, she was spotted one day by a local journalist wearing rather outrageous attire.

"She was dressed in high heels, black pants, an animal print jacket and puffed-up hair," reported Scott Doughlas. "I thought to myself, 'That's

J. K. Rowling. She's obviously got a vampish side.' "

Unfortunately the price of fame would soon cause Joanne some discomfort. With her worldwide popularity, she found herself the target of overzealous and obsessed fans, whose attention and correspondence regarding her every waking moment became unsettling. Sadly, with the protection of her family and herself uppermost in her thoughts, Joanne, in 2002, had eight-foot-high walls, topped with electrified fencing, built around her home.

But things were not all strident and serious in those months. Long a fan of *The Simpsons* television series, Joanne was approached by the show's creator, Matt Groening, to appear in an episode of *The Simpsons* that had the cartoon family traveling to England and running into J. K. Rowling at a bookstore, where they exchange comic pleasantries with the author. Joanne readily agreed and had quite a bit of fun recording her dialogue for the episode, entitled *The Regina Monologues*, which aired late in 2003 to rave reviews.

In her final month of pregnancy, Joanne continued to be encouraged by the reports she was receiving about the earliest days of filming *Harry Potter and the Prisoner of Azkaban*. Filming had officially begun on February 24 at Leavesden Studio in London and would continue to film in lavish outdoor locations in London and Scotland. Joining the returning cast from the previous films were newcomers Gary Oldman, who plays Sirius Black, Michael Gambon as Professor Dumbledore, Timothy Spall as Peter Pettigrew, David Thewlis as Professor Lupin, Pam Ferris as Aunt Marge, and Paul Whitehouse as Sir Caddogan.

As production began, director Alfonso Cuarón beamed with pride as he told the press, "To be entrusted with such rich and beloved material and to be given the opportunity to collaborate with this extraordinary cast and crew on the next Harry Potter adventure is an honor. I look forward to bringing this intricate story to the screen and sharing it with film audiences around the world."

The enormity of the production, with its trademark special effects and scenes with literally hundreds of extras in them, was going to be a long, complex production. And so, although the first two films had been right on time for a Christmas release, the studio knew better than to rush the film out. It was announced early in the production that *Harry Potter and the Prisoner of Azkaban* would not be released until early 2004 (perhaps February or March) but most likely not until May or June 2004.

The past year, which Joanne would describe in a *Sunday Herald* interview as "hellish and massively stressful," had given way to a period of quiet reflection and solitude as Joanne waited for the blessed event. She was already working on early elements of the sixth Harry Potter book but was finding it difficult to focus on the task at hand. In a rare correspondence with a fan, *WizardNews.com* reported that Joanne told a young child, "It's really strange writing the book now that I'm pregnant."

But while her obligations to Harry continued to demand her attention, Joanne was, overall, in a comfortable state during her last months of pregnancy. According to an interview with Barbara Murray, Neil's mother, in *People,* "She is relaxed and glowing. She's looking so very happy with the new baby coming and the marriage going so well."

Those in her immediate circle knew that, despite the marriage, the coming baby, and the worldwide notoriety that continued to grow because of the success of her books, very little had changed in Joanne's life.

"Rowling still has her feet on the ground," reflected her publicist Rosamund de la Hey in a *People* article. "Her life has changed very little in day-to-day ways, apart from the obvious financial security she now has."

Shortly after the first of the year, Joanne's publisher announced that *Harry Potter and the Order of the Phoenix* would be in stores on June 21, 2003. Not long after that announcement was made, Joanne went into labor.

Joanne was driven by Neil to the New Royal Infirmary's Simpson Center for Reproductive Health on Sunday, March 24. Not long after entering the hospital, David Gordon Rowling Murray, weighing in at a little more than eight pounds, was born. The birth of Joanne's second child was of worldwide interest, but it was the local Scotland papers, such as the *Edinburgh Evening News,* who were there first with all the facts.

Shortly after the birth, Nicky Stonehill, speaking for Rowling, announced the birth and added, "Both mother and baby were doing well."

Neil's mother, Barbara Murray, was one of the first to talk publicly about the birth of her grandchild when she was quoted in the *Edinburgh Evening News* as saying, "I've seen David and he is gaining weight, more than eight pounds at the moment. Both Joanne and the baby are doing well. We're all just highly delighted."

After a short recuperation period, Joanne and the baby were brought home by proud father Neil amid tight security around the home. The few friends and family members who were allowed into the home to see the newborn had to pass through a checkpoint in which names were matched with a very short list of who would be allowed inside.

Joanne had already stated that she would not go through the kind of publicity with an *Order of the Phoenix* tour that had accompanied her last book, and so, with the birth of David, it was announced by her publisher that she was planning on making fewer press appearances and that there would be no long book tours. An official statement from her publisher further stated that the baby would only be three months old when the book was published and, like any new mother, she wanted to enjoy the time. In a related press statement, Joanne said, "It's a very important time for me and my husband and we want to spend as much of it as we can with the baby and Jessica."

Joanne spent the next few weeks largely in seclusion, spending almost all her waking hours with the baby. Her natural loving, mothering instincts were very much in evidence as she soothingly cooed to the baby and comforted her bundle of joy. Their quiet moments together were often taken up with long walks through the mansion. Joanne would stop, look out a window, and introduce her young son to the world around her. At that moment, work was the farthest thing from her mind.

But her absence from the public eye did not prevent the world of Harry Potter from continuing to turn.

Joanne's U.S. publisher, Scholastic, in their summer preview catalog, unveiled the plot synopsis of *Harry Potter and the Order of the Phoenix*. It read: "Lord Voldemort's rise has opened a rift in the wizarding world between those who believe the truth about his return and those who prefer to believe that it is all just madness and lies. Harry confronts the unreliability of the government of the magical world and the impotence of the authorities of Hogwarts."

In April, a press conference covered by BBC and other media outlets was assembled to announce the release of the *Harry Potter and the Chamber of Secrets* DVD. But as is often true of these kinds of events, the real news was the tidbits of information that were revealed about the Harry Potter movies to come.

Film producer David Heyman announced that *Harry Potter and the Prisoner of Azkaban* had been in production in and around London and the British countryside since February and that the production was right on schedule. As an example of what Harry Potter fans could look forward to on the big screen, Heyman explained how the film company had recently completed a scene in the Gryffindor Common Room where Professor McGonagall is angry at Neville after finding out that he had left the password list lying around.

Robbie Coltraine, who had played Hagrid in the previous two Harry Potter movies, said that there was something new on the horizon for his character in the new film. "Hagrid has a new look," he said at the press conference. "He's got a waistcoat. His clothes are looking more like he made them himself, which, indeed, I'm sure he did."

Producer Heyman also revealed that writer Steve Kloves was already hard at work on the script for *Harry Potter and the Goblet of Fire*. He indicated that while that script was being written with the idea of it being one movie, there was the possibility that, because of the length and complex nature of the story, there was a very real chance that *Goblet of Fire* might end up being made into two movies. Heyman reported that *Goblet of Fire* would most likely go before the cameras sometime in 2004, and that the movie would be released a year to a year and a half after the release of the third film.

Uppermost in the minds of many has been the fact that the child stars of the Harry Potter films were getting older and that there might be a point when the actors will have outgrown the part. Heyman addressed the question of whether *Prisoner of Azkaban* might be the last time in Harry Potter's world for Daniel Radcliffe, Emma Watson, and Rupert Grint.

"My hope is that it would be the same cast. But it's too early to tell, though."

Another rumor, addressed by Chris Columbus at the press conference, was whether the director of the first two Harry Potter movies would be back to direct the fourth. Columbus, who bowed out of directing *Prisoner of Azkaban* to spend more time with his family, indicated that while "Four was starting a little too quickly, five is a possibility."

By early May, the completed manuscript for *Harry Potter and the Order of the Phoenix* had been edited and, amid tight security measures that one usually associates with a visit from royalty, the page proofs were driven to the printing plant, Clays Ltd., in the nearby town of Suffolk, where the first issues of Joanne's new book would be printed. Rumors, almost as fantastic as Joanne's books, began to circulate.

One widely reported rumor had it that crates containing the new books would not be delivered until the day before the publication date and that the books would be brought in by armed guards. One story that was much reported was that, after the book was edited, Joanne and her publisher reportedly sent sketches of what they wanted the book jacket to look like to the cover artist, Jason Cockscroft, rather than letting him see the book and generate his own ideas. One person who did get an advance look at the book was Mary Grand

Pré, who created the illustrations for inside the book and had to read the entire story before she did her work.

Around this time there was rabid speculation about whether Joanne had let Neil or her daughter Jessica get a sneak peak at the book. Many assumed that both her husband and her daughter had been monitoring the work in progress and may well have read some, if not all of the book already. But nobody could be sure.

Review copies to influential reviewers were also being handed out with extreme care and with the warning that there might be dire consequences if reviews ran too soon or if too much of the story was given away too far in advance of the publication date.

For many, these precautions might appear to be a bit much. However, with the worldwide popularity of Harry Potter, there had emerged, with recent books, stories of people attempting to steal copies of the manuscripts and sell them to certain media outlets, thus destroying the surprise for devoted readers. Joanne had no problem with these precautions.

But despite the security, Joanne's worst fear would come true during the second week of May 2003.

Keith Webb, a truck driver, was walking through a field in Suffolk when he happened to look down and spotted what appeared to be a couple of old, coverless, discarded books. In an interview with the *Sun* newspaper, Webb would relate what happened next.

"I wondered what it was and bent down to pick them up. I was astonished when I read the front page and saw that it was copies of the latest Harry Potter book."

What had tipped Webb off was that the first page contained the title *Harry Potter and the Order of the Phoenix* and Joanne's name. Webb also saw that the dedication page read "To Neil, David and Jessica who make my world magical."

Surprisingly, Webb's first thought was to call the *Sun* and report his finding. Webb eventually turned the copies of the book over to the newspaper. Even more surprising was the action of the *Sun,* a paper often known for dabbling in gossip and sensationalism. The newspaper editors locked the books up for safe keeping, would not let anybody read them, and called Joanne's publisher to come and get them.

When Joanne heard the news she was at first extremely upset and then relieved when she was told that the books had been returned, apparently unread. However, her concerns resurfaced when it was reported that the *Sun* and several other publications had received mysterious telephone calls from someone offering to sell them the first three chapters of the new book for a large amount of money. The publications all refused the offer, but there remained the fear that at least one other copy of *Order of the Phoenix* was in the hands of somebody who was trying to ruin the surprises the new book had to offer.

The Suffolk police stepped in and began investigating the apparent theft of the copies of the book from the printer. There was a collective sigh of relief a few days later when a forty-four-year-old man was arrested and charged with stealing copies of chapters of the novel and a pair of teenage boys were arrested and charged with handling stolen goods.

Joanne was sorry that these people had used the idea of making money to enter into a life of crime. But she was relieved to discover that millions of children would not have the surprise of opening *Harry Potter and the Order of the Phoenix* and reading those first pages taken from them. Once more she reflected on the price of fame and the occasional bad things that were done in connection with her work. Unfortunately, there was little she could do to prevent these things from happening, and so she chose to put the negative things out of her mind and concentrate on all the good things.

As the days counted down to the June 21 release date of *Harry Potter and the Order of the Phoenix,* bookstores around the world prepared for the new book with a variety of in-store parties and readings centered around the world of Harry Potter. Many stores had arranged to begin selling copies of the new book at the stroke of midnight. Joanne continued to state that she would do very few press appearances. And what she would do, while not on the scale of her massive reading in Canada years earlier, would be for the benefit of children.

Joanne agreed that on June 26, five days after the publication of *Harry Potter and the Order of the Phoenix,* she would appear at the famous Royal Albert Hall in London to read from and answer questions regarding her latest book. The audience would be made up of 4,000 children who would be selected through a contest run by both her British and U.S. publishers.

But beyond that appearance, Joanne was insistent that they would see little of her or her new baby, who, nearing two months old, was nowhere near ready to be out in public.

The weather in Scotland in May can go from sunny and warm to rainy and cold in the blink of an eye. Nowhere was this more apparent than in the rolling hills and deep forests of Glencoe in northern Scotland, where much of *Harry Potter and the Prisoner of Azkaban* was being filmed.

Outdoor scenes in which the Executioner pays a visit to Hagrid's Hut had to be postponed for three days because of rain. The resourceful filmmakers got around this act of God by filming the interior elements of these sequences at nearby Fort Williams. When the rain finally gave way to sunshine, director Cuarón moved the production back outside where, over the course of a number of days, they filmed the aforementioned scenes around Hagrid's Hut and, with the film's three stars leading well over a hundred child extras, a number of scenes involving Hogwarts Castle were also completed.

David turned two months old at the end of May. It was a time of happiness and quiet expectation. In a relatively short time, Neil had grown to be the ideal father, attentive to the needs of his son and eager to spend time alone with him when Joanne needed to rest or some time to write. Jessica adored her younger brother and would spend every free hour playing childlike make-believe games.

Joanne was continuing to work on the sixth Harry Potter book but was doing so at a more leisurely pace. No longer willing to race through the ever more complex storylines in an attempt to satisfy her publisher's need for a new book every year, Joanne had publicly announced that she would be taking more time with the next book and that readers will most likely have to wait until sometime in the year 2005 for the next Harry Potter adventure. There was some disappointment when Joanne made that announcement, but most of her fans eventually came to realize that they had to be patient in order to get the best Harry story that Joanne could possibly write.

Joanne was feeling a wide variety of emotions as she realized that, in writing the sixth Harry Potter adventure, she was nearly finished with the promised seven-book odyssey. By the time that last book was completed, Harry would be eighteen years old and ready to go out into the world. And what of Joanne at that point? Materially she would never want for anything and could, if she desired, stop writing and never have to work again. But Joanne often rationalized that writers live to write and, while she did not know for sure what she would do after Harry, she was sure that she would be writing something.

Harry Potter mania began to shift into high gear during the early days of June. Bookstores and Web sites were counting down the days, the hours, and, yes, even the seconds. Newspapers and magazines were filled with stories covering every aspect of Joanne and the arrival of her latest work. One story proclaimed that at the stroke of midnight on June 20, nearly 9 million copies of *Harry Potter and the Order of the Phoenix* would be released in the United States alone. A report from Ireland indicated that sales of the coming new book would easily outdistance sales of the Bible. A library in Oregon made worldwide news when they reported ordering 700 copies of *Harry Potter and the Order of the Phoenix* in order to accommodate the more than one thousand requests that had already come in to check out the book.

Joanne continued to be amazed at the amount of attention being put on her creation. But then she would hear the cries of her child, who craved attention on a level that only a mother could understand; it was at moments like that that Joanne knew what was important.

One of the more amazing things to Joanne were the recent polls conducted in England and Scotland that focused on the most powerful and/or rich people in the land. In a poll conducted by the Sunday *Times,* Joanne found herself near the top of a list of the wealthiest people in England, an astounding eleven places higher than Queen Elizabeth. And in a list of Scotland's most powerful 100 people, Joanne came in at number four.

Joanne told a reporter that she would look at these lists and find it hard to believe that she was on them. In many ways that person was not real to her. After all, just a few short years ago, she had been a single mother living on welfare in a drafty flat. Now she had mansions and a loving family around her. Joanne knew it was a fantasy come true. But she also prided herself that with all the accolades that had come her way because of Harry, she had kept to her values. She knew that money and power had caused many people to change for the worst once they had come into the public spotlight. And she knew that she had not become one of those people.

Joanne agreed to do a few interviews in the weeks and days leading up to the publication of *Harry Potter and the Order of the Phoenix.* Because of the nature of the interviews she had done on the release of her previous four books, Joanne had come to expect a certain line of questioning that she felt more than capable of answering. But she soon realized that a lot had happened in the previous two years. So while a good part of the interviews centered around the new book, a lot was asked about her new baby, her husband, and many other things she considered highly personal. True to her private nature, Joanne would respond to those questions with vague or simplistic answers, refusing to go into any grand detail. She was grateful that even the more gossip-oriented reporters did not push her hard for personal information, and even happier to find that the often jaded reporters maintained a high degree of enthusiasm for the coming of *Harry Potter and the Order of the Phoenix.*

With all the incredible excitement surrounding the coming release of *Order of the Phoenix* that often, reasoned Joanne, seemed to focus more on the material aspects of the books than the joys inherent in the stories themselves, she was quite heartened to discover that one of her many fans was turning his interest in Harry Potter to charitable use. Adam Orton, a fifteen-year-old English lad, had raised more than 1,000 pounds for the Children's Liver Disease Foundation by auctioning off several signed Harry Potter books.

During this period, Joanne continued to get progress reports on the filming of *Harry Potter and the Prisoner of Azkaban* in nearby Glencoe. And the reports were not always good. An unexpected fire had halted the proceedings for several days, plus rain, mud, and the constant presence of flies had resulted in the production being two weeks behind schedule. At one point, things got so bad that the actors had to be transported to a hilltop location in a snowmobile. To make matters worse, filming in and around the outdoor location of Hogwarts bridge had become so bad that the entire prop bridge had to be taken down and rebuilt inside a London soundstage.

Still, she was heartened to learn that, despite these setbacks, a firm release date for the film of June 4, 2004, had been announced. On the other hand, she was quite surprised that it was already being stated in many press outlets that Warner Bros. was planning on making two movies out of the sixth Harry Potter book. The sixth book was nowhere near completion, so Joanne was curious as to how such a statement could be made. But she did not let these stories get in the way of her life and her work.

Joanne continued to be consumed with David. It had been a number of years since she had dealt with the everyday requirements of a newborn, and she was finding unbelievable joy in the most mundane of moments. The chores of feeding, cuddling, and changing helped fill her days and settle her nerves as she anticipated the arrival of her next blessed event. Joanne had, by this time, become accustomed to all the attention that came along with the publication of each new Harry Potter book and, she reflected, nothing could ever erase the memory of the publicity tour that accompanied the release of *Harry Potter and the Goblet of Fire.*

But a lot of questions had been asked this time around of her and her creation, and Joanne admitted to herself that *Harry Potter and the Order of the Phoenix* was a turning point for her characters and her career. The adventures of Harry would end in a relatively short time, and then she would be faced with the question of what she would do with the rest of her life. Although she felt confident that the new book would be a smashing success, she was already looking to the future. . . .

And it was a future in which she did not have all the answers.

Finally the day arrived. The world had been counting down for months, then weeks, then days, then hours. Around the world lines were beginning to form outside bookstores: anxious children and just as anxious parents. Inside, the books were being piled high, their jackets aligned to welcome fans to Joanne's continuing fantasy.

At the stroke of midnight on June 20, 2003, the doors opened. Minutes into the new day, millions of readers were already opening the book. The adventure was once again beginning to unfold. Despite her insistence that she would not do any appearances other than the Royal Albert Hall reading, Joanne, on the day *Order of the Phoenix* was published, had an unexpected change of heart and, shortly after the books went on sale, appeared unannounced at a local Edinburgh bookstore where she happily signed copies of her new book and talked to the surprised and delighted children.

Harry fans were so excited that they could not wait to get the book home and were sitting, alone or in clusters, reading silently, or standing in excited twos and threes around the bookstore. It soon became an informal contest to see who could read the book the fastest, with a young college student reportedly finishing the book in 104 minutes. Over the next days, there would be endless stories surrounding the publication of the book. The first reviews were not long in coming and were all fairly unanimous in their praise of the book, making particular notation of the complexity and depth of the story and the believable way in which Harry and his companions had grown up. It was also touched on, in a positive sense, that *Order of the Phoenix* was the darkest book yet.

All available copies of *Harry Potter and the Or-*

der of the Phoenix were quickly snapped up and, despite the thousands of copies ordered by many stores in preparation, many soon found themselves running low or completely out of copies of the book in a matter of days and were placing frantic orders for more books to keep up with the demand. The printers were working around the clock, printing up more and more copies in an attempt to keep up with the worldwide outcry for more books.

Much controversy and debate surfaced when it was discovered that it was Sirius Black, a close friend of Harry's, who was killed. But finally the long anticipated death was felt to be a satisfactory, albeit unpleasant decision.

Joanne was thrilled with the response and not just the slightest bit relieved as she received the good news that her book had immediately jumped to number one on a number of the most prestigious bestseller lists. But it did not take long for her nervousness to return when she realized that her reading at the Royal Albert Hall was only a few days away.

Joanne had been forced to overcome her shyness in promoting the previous books, and she looked back in pride on her ability to command an audience of thousands in the Canadian sports stadium and in smaller but equally crowded rooms during the promotion of the last book. Now, some of the old fears and discomfort of speaking in public had returned, but, once she reminded herself that she would be speaking in front of children who were her biggest supporters, she felt calmer.

Still, she remained in an excited state on the day she traveled to London for the Royal Albert Hall appearance. She rarely went into London except for business reasons, and so she was once again enchanted by the sights and sounds that greeted her.

She was not surprised to find that the scene outside the hall was similar to those that had followed her every public appearance since Harry Potter had put her in the public eye. Thousands of children and, yes, adults, were being politely but firmly held back behind barricades by the local police. Many in attendance were dressed as their favorite Harry Potter character and many held copies of the new book. Through an elaborate security setup, those lucky children who had won coveted tickets to the event were being allowed in.

Joanne entered Royal Albert Hall through a

backstage entrance and then she waited in the wings for a formal introduction. As she looked out into the packed hall, memories of her last big appearance in Canada surely came rushing back to her. While on a much smaller scale, the Royal Albert Hall was electric with excitement as children from places all over the map chattered excitedly as they embraced this special moment and awaited Joanne's appearance. The hall had been done up to look like Hogwarts and ushers were dressed in Harry Potter style robes in keeping with the occasion.

Just when it seemed that the noise level could not get any higher, Joanne was introduced. Screams and cheers of joy greeted Joanne as she walked to center stage. She smiled, a deep, satisfied smile. Any sense of nervousness melted away as 4,000 children expressed their love for her and what she had brought to their lives.

Joanne thanked them for coming and, after a few introductory comments, commenced to read a passage from *Harry Potter and the Order of the Phoenix*. Many in the audience had their own copies of the book open to the appropriate page and were reading along silently, and, in some cases, aloud. Another round of applause and cheers roared up as Joanne looked up from her book, finishing her reading.

Joanne followed up the reading by answering questions from the moderator and from the audience. She would later acknowledge in an interview that she was amazed at the earnestness of the questions. They wanted to know why this book had taken so long to write, why she had decided to take characters in the directions she did, what the future books would be like, and what she thought of the movies. There was also the occasional question about the new baby and her family, which, since they were coming from children rather than the press, she answered.

Joanne left the stage to thunderous applause. The children were the people for whom she wrote the Harry Potter books. This demonstration of their approval of what she had done was all the praise that she needed.

Now it was back to the warmth and comfort of her family.

With the uproar over her latest book continuing, Joanne retreated to a simple home life, taking care of baby David, looking after the needs of Neil and Jessica, and, for the first time in a long time, writing without the pressure of deadlines. After the stress she suffered writing *Goblet of Fire* and *Order of the Phoenix* literally back to back, Joanne came to an agreement with her publishers that the last two books would be delivered in their own time.

Although mum on the particulars of her current progress, Joanne did tell the London *Times* that "book six will be shorter than *Order of the Phoenix* but that the final book would most likely be massive." Joanne was also quite happy with the reports that the movie version of *Harry Potter and the Prisoner of Azkaban* had survived the numerous delays in Glencoe and was now right on schedule for its summer 2004 release.

With her personal life now very much a priority and the professional pressures of the past couple of years behind her, Joanne had emerged a complete, fulfilled woman who continues to make it her mission to bring the joys of Harry Potter into the lives of millions.

"Ultimately I need to do this," she recently told the London *Times*. "I could have stopped writing four years ago and I would have been fine financially. At this point in my life I'm not writing for the money and I could definitely do without the fame. The only point is to satisfy myself now and out of loyalty to the fans. But when I say it's for me, it's also for Harry . . . and being true to what I know will be his end."

15

THE GHOST AT THE WINDOW

J oanne found herself in a state of grace midway through 2003. She was very much in a family way, as she spent waking hours dealing with the needs of her now four-month-old son, David. She watched, often in amusement, as her daughter, Jessica, blossomed into a bright and precocious preteen. Her husband, Neil—the always supportive, understanding, and loving man she had fallen in love with—remained a rock in her eyes.

Truth be told, in Neil Joanne had found the perfect life partner in her much-celebrated life.

From the beginning, Neil had been interested in her and not her celebrity and wealth. He continued to be a conscientious worker in his own occupation, and his long hours often matched or surpassed those of Joanne. And like Joanne's, his tastes were simple and nonmaterialistic. Joanne had found her Prince Charming.

Jessica continued to be a supportive and understanding daughter; often laughing off the notoriety that followed her mother and, despite the attention focused on her because of her mother, was living a fairly normal life.

Joanne was content. But her writer's mind continued to work, thinking about where her creation Harry Potter and his wondrous world would venture next. Joanne recalled that she had, in fact, started pulling the elements of *Harry Potter and the Half-Blood Prince* together while she had been pregnant with David. But the demands of motherhood caused her to put the book aside once her son was born. At this moment, she was not in any hurry to return to the book. Joanne had made it plain to both publishers and fans alike that the rapid pace in which the first five Harry Potter books were written had stopped. Her family life was now her priority and those hungry for the next adventure would have to wait.

"I took a break at one point because I had been working very hard for about eight or nine years and partly because I wanted to spend time with my children," she explained in a CBBC press conference. "If I lose fans because of the wait, then I guess I just have to take it on the chin."

However, she was already thinking in terms of the storyline and characters that would finally jump from the pages of the sixth Harry Potter novel, *Harry Potter and the Half-Blood Prince.*

Joanne has always been her own worst critic when it came to Harry Potter. She has often said that *Harry Potter and the Order of the Phoenix* was too long and that *Harry Potter and the Goblet of Fire* was overpraised. And she knew that *Harry Potter and the Half-Blood Prince,* with its emphasis on evil and the family, would be an important element as the Harry Potter series neared its end.

"I really planned out this one," she recalled in an interview with *Time* magazine. "I took three months and just sat there and went over and over the plan. I really fine-tuned it. I looked at it from every angle. I had learned from my past mistakes."

Joanne began writing *Harry Potter and the Half-Blood Prince* shortly before the New Year and, by early 2004, was by her own definition "well into the book." As has been her custom in recent years, Joanne's writing room featured a large detailed wall chart propped up on her desk. The chart contained bits of information about what happened to which characters at what point in the book and where all important clues might be slipped into seemingly unimportant moments of the book.

Joanne would often say that writing *Harry Potter and the Half-Blood Prince* was probably one of the more relaxing writing periods she had in her life. When the needs of Neil, Jessica, and David were uppermost, she could put Harry aside for the moment and return at her leisure and not miss a beat.

However, the ease of the writing was balanced out by the awareness, perhaps for the first time, that her creation was nearing its end. She often commented during this period that so much of what happens in book six relates to book seven that it almost appeared as if she were writing two halves of the same novel.

"The original plan for the series has changed along the way, but only in details," she said at a

2005 question-and-answer session at the Edinburgh Book Festival. "The story has taken little twists and turns that maybe I didn't expect. Each book has done what it was supposed to do in taking you towards the final conclusion."

Joanne's reputation as a fantasy author of the first order would occasionally lead to writing offers outside the realm of Harry Potter. One such offer came in the midst of writing *Half-Blood Prince,* when the producer of the returning British television series *Dr. Who* had given Joanne the opportunity to write a script for that show's first season. Joanne politely turned down the opportunity on the grounds that she was just too busy with the latest Harry Potter book to consider other writing jobs.

Joanne had gotten used to doing her writing in the room of her castle. But she would occasionally get restless and, during the writing of *Harry Potter and the Half-Blood Prince,* sneak out to various restaurants and coffee shops and write over a steaming cup of coffee at an out-of-the-way outdoor table. But a lot had changed since Joanne had written the first Harry Potter novel at a table at Nicholson's Café. Joanne had become a fairly recognizable figure on the streets of Edinburgh over the years, and she was now finding it next to impossible to hide in plain sight. Sometimes she would be able to steal away for a couple of hours to write at an outdoor café, but often she would look up from her pad to find a group of people staring at her. Joanne took the interruptions in good nature and, even though it would inevitably cut short the writing sessions, she was comforted by the memories of the simple times before she became the most popular writer on the planet.

In April 2004, Joanne discovered that she was pregnant.

Neil and Joanne were ecstatic at the prospect of adding to their family. Three children had always seemed like the right number for Joanne. Word quickly spread around the world that Joanne was going to have another baby. Letters and e-mail congratulating the couple on the blessed event were followed by both press and fan inquiries as to how the months of pregnancy would impact the completion of the latest Harry Potter book. Joanne attempted to address those concerns in several statements in which she said while she could not say for sure when the book would be completed, she did not see her pregnancy disrupting her normal writing schedule.

And, as the months moved forward, Joanne found that she was fairly able to balance out impending motherhood, the needs of her family, and writing a blockbuster novel without missing a beat.

She conceded in a 2005 CBBC news conference that having a young family had cut down on the number of ten-hour writing days and especially her favorite pastime, writing all night. She also reported during that session that her pregnancy during the writing of *Harry Potter and the Half-Blood Prince* had caused her to vary her writing schedule somewhat.

"I think at the end of *Half-Blood Prince,* I was certainly writing eight hours a day. I would have been doing longer but, at that point, I was very heavily pregnant and there comes a point, when you are absolutely huge, that you have to get up and walk around a while because it literally gets uncomfortable."

While working on *Half-Blood Prince,* Joanne was constantly receiving reports on preparation for the start of production on the film adaptation of

Harry Potter and the Goblet of Fire. She was delighted to find that an Englishman, Mike Newell, had been chosen to direct the film, and that Steve Kloves would continue as the only screenwriter on the Harry Potter film series. Joanne was also happy to hear that, despite rumors that the three leads might be replaced because they had gotten too old, Daniel Radcliffe, Rupert Grint, and Emma Watson would return in the roles of Harry Potter, Ron Weasley, and Hermione Granger. Filming was scheduled to begin in England in June.

She was also keeping up on reports of the film version of her book *Harry Potter and the Prisoner of Azkaban.* Director Alfonso Cuarón had originally been thought of as a risky choice to bring the latest Harry Potter adventure to the screen, but as the months progressed he had proven himself an imaginative interpreter of Joanne's fantasy world. Originally scheduled for an early 2004 release, *Harry Potter and the Prisoner of Azkaban* was now officially on track for a June 4, 2004, release date.

In early May 2004, Joanne was notified that the film was officially completed and was invited to a screening for select press and studio executives. As with the previous films, Joanne was nervous at the prospect of seeing this third Harry Potter adventure up on the big screen. But as the lights went down and the first images flickered onto the screen, a satisfied smile crossed Joanne's face and stayed in place until the final credits rolled at the end of the film.

"I've been happy with all the films," recalled Joanne in a question-and-answer session at the 2005 Edinburgh Book Festival. "Of the three, *Azkaban* is my favorite. I thought it was really good for a lot of different reasons. I thought that Alfonso Cuarón, the director, did a fantastic job and that Dan, Emma, and Rupert were really wonderful in the film."

By this time, Joanne had also gotten used to the reality that the films would not be same as her books, and was comfortable with how the film industry was interpreting Harry.

"I guess if you did every scene in the book, the films would be twenty-four hours each," she said in a CBBC press conference. "So they have got to prune and change things slightly. But by and large they meet my expectations."

Joanne had a chance to see the film for a second time a few weeks later when she attended the official London premiere of *Harry Potter and the Prisoner of Azkaban.* Joanne was a little girl at heart when it came to the glitz and glamour of a big movie premiere. The film gave her an even bigger sense of joy as she sat with a star-studded celebrity audience and heard their applause and shouts of appreciation as the film unfolded.

Later, at the post-screening party, Joanne got to meet the actors Gary Oldman, David Thewlis, and Michael Gambon, whose performances had done so much for the movies. She also met Dan, Emma, and Rupert for the first time in a while and openly marveled at how the three children had matured into attractive young men and women over the course of the three Harry Potter films.

As work progressed on *Half-Blood Prince,* the expected rumors and wild speculations once again began swirling around Joanne and her creation. Stories began to appear that indicated a major character would die. There were reports of people going through her garbage in hopes of finding a hint of information about the upcoming book. Bribes were reportedly offered to those close to Joanne for any and all information.

The ongoing attention of the tabloid press was

also a bother. Pictures of her out and about were an annoyance she could tolerate. However, when pictures of Jessica began to appear in newspapers and magazines, Joanne decided she would have to go to extraordinary lengths to have privacy for her family and herself. When the family decided on a trip to Hawaii, they hired a private jet. A trip to a South African safari camp was also accomplished under a cloak of secrecy. For an extravagant party to celebrate her fortieth birthday, Joanne booked the party, location, and all the details of her celebration under her married name of Mrs. Murray.

The constant attention of the worldwide press had reached the point where she now dreamed of the days when her life was much simpler and she was a struggling unknown rather than, reportedly, the richest writer in the world.

Joanne's longing for a less complicated life manifested itself midway through 2005, when Neil and she were taking some time off in Edinburgh and happened to find themselves in a part of the city they had never gone to before. Suddenly Joanne realized that they were very close to the flat where she, as a struggling single mother, had written *Harry Potter and the Philosopher's Stone*. With the first response to that book, Joanne had left the flat and had moved into a new house. Over the years, she had never expressed a desire to return to the place. But now she impulsively said to Neil that the place where she used to live was right around the corner and that they should go take a look.

"When I clapped eyes on the place, I burst into tears," she said in an interview with *Dateline NBC*. "I couldn't stop crying. For a moment, I was back where I had been all these years ago. It brought back this tidal wave of emotion. And I think it hit me so hard how life had changed. And, in all respects, how wonderful it was."

With Neil at her side, Joanne continued to stare at the cramped room that she used to call home. A wave of emotions washed over her. "I'm looking at this place and I'm thinking that it was almost like I would see the ghost of myself standing in the window and I would be able to communicate with that person," she revealed to *Dateline*. " 'It's all going to be okay, you're working so hard and it will be okay.' I will never forget how it felt to go back there."

As 2005 neared its conclusion, the press were

constantly on the alert for something of note on Joanne's life and work. More than one columnist speculated on whether the writer's third child or the sixth book would come first. The reality was that Joanne, despite the growing discomfort in the final months of her pregnancy, was working at a brisk pace to finish the book. Neil and Jessica were of great help during this period, helping with emotional and physical support as Joanne finished *Harry Potter and the Half-Blood Prince* shortly before the end of 2004.

Joanne went into labor on January 23, 2005, and the couple's third child, named Mackenzie Jean Rowling Murray, was born. Neil and Joanne were thrilled with their new arrival and withdrew from the public eye to welcome the new addition to their family home. At the same time the publishing world was making plans of its own; to make the latest addition to Joanne's creative family the biggest seller yet.

16

COUNTDOWN TO SIX

July 16, 2005, had been selected for the official publication date of *Harry Potter and the Half-Blood Prince*. Joanne's publishers were planning on making history with book six. A planned first-edition run of 10.8 million books would make *Half-Blood Prince* the largest first-edition run of any book in the history of publishing.

Like previous books, extraordinary security measures were being taken to avoid any secrets of *Half-Blood Prince* being revealed. Armed guards were to be deployed around any print shops and binderies where the book was to be put together. ID badges would be required for anyone going anywhere that even a page of the manuscript might be visible.

The intense amount of security had also seeped into Joanne's life as well. She had long ago taken to locking up her work in her office and, more recently, had started shredding any notes or pages that might fall into the hands of the press. Joanne had even begun to censor herself during interviews, fearful that anything she said would instantly make its way onto the Internet and be analyzed and discussed.

Joanne commented on the sheer madness of it all in an interview with *Dateline NBC*. "I sometimes feel that the world has gone insane. I mean ultimately what is this? It's a kids' book. I mean obviously it's my life and I've worked very hard on it. I think all of this is just surreal."

Joanne continued to pull back from the public as the countdown to book six commenced, devoting herself to the needs of her family and, in particular, the by now slightly more than a year-old David and newborn Mackenzie. Joanne was managing to get some writing time in but it was tempered by the attention being paid to her family.

"I have three children now so I am quite good at prioritizing my time," she said in a CBBC press conference. "I no longer write five days a week. Sometimes I'll write two and a half days a week. I sort of work around my children so I spend a lot of time with them."

Any concern that more than two years between books would dampen the interest of young readers in *Harry Potter and the Half-Blood Prince* was ended when, months before the publication of the book, bookstores in both the United States and England reported more than two hundred thousand advance orders for the book. Stores around the world were already planning theme parties centered around the latest Harry Potter adventure. And as the days and weeks counted down, Joanne was finding herself dealing with rumors surrounding the book that had seemed to take on a life of their own.

Internet sites, claiming to have somehow gotten a copy of the book, were claiming that certain characters, including reportedly Harry himself, died in the book. Some fan sites were displaying e-mails, allegedly sent by Joanne, in which story secrets were revealed. Many online sites claimed to have signed copies of *Half-Blood Prince* available for sale.

Ever considerate of the feelings of her readers, Joanne responded to the rumors on her own Web site. In part she stated: "I have been alerted to the fact that I am supposed to have posted in the comments section of a couple of different fan sites recently. I never post on fan sites and it is important that you all know this. The last thing I would want is for any of you to be misled or otherwise manipulated by somebody posing as me online."

While she had barely completed work on *Harry Potter and the Half-Blood Prince*, Joanne, unbeknownst to most, was already doing some mental preparation for what would be the seventh and final Harry Potter book. She conceded that she did have a plan but had not, as yet, plotted the book out chapter by chapter. Joanne would not suggest that the final book would be as long as her previous novels, but she did not rule out the possibility that the final book might truly be massive. One thing was sure, and that was that the final book in the

Harry Potter odyssey would take as long to write as it took her to write it.

"I think it will be at least another two-year wait," she disclosed in a 2005 CBBC press conference. "I'm just being realistic. My plan is to start writing seriously at the end of the year because I still have a very young baby. But I am doing some work on it at the moment."

The pre-publicity campaign for the release of *Harry Potter and the Half-Blood Prince* was now shifting into motion. Joanne was dealing with countless suggestions from publishers and publicists on how best to promote the new book. Joanne liked the idea of something big and splashy to kick off the campaign.

But the one thing she did not want was a repeat of the cross-country train ride that had marked the release of *Harry Potter and the Goblet of Fire*. Joanne had enjoyed the train trip and the opportunity to meet with children at every stop. However, in looking back on that event, what stuck out most in her mind was that, more often than not, the children she most wanted to interact with were relegated to second-class status amid the rush of the press. After some thought, the writer came up with a plan that would involve the children who had been her most ardent fans and a sense of bigger than life fantasy.

Bloomsbury, Joanne's British publisher, came up with the idea of the writer doing her first official press conference for the new book in front of a group of young children who, through various contests and based on their knowledge of the Harry Potter universe, would be chosen. Joanne loved the idea, feeling that it would allow her the kind of direct contact with her readers that she had not had in years.

The next challenge was to find a place to hold the event. Not wanting to venture too far from home, Joanne came up with the idea of holding the event in centuries-old Edinburgh Castle. Joanne felt the castle would be the perfect backdrop for this party. The castle also struck a nostalgic tone with Joanne as it was in the city where she wrote the first Harry Potter novel.

With the castle as a backdrop, the publication party quickly grew to encompass three days of Hogwarts-style merriment.

The final week before the official unveiling of *Harry Potter and the Half-Blood Prince* reflected the heightened sense of security that had surrounded the delivery of previous Harry Potter novels. Books were delivered in heavily guarded trucks in securely bound boxes. There were specific instructions that books were not to be sold until the stroke of midnight on July 16. But despite the publisher's best efforts, a bookstore in Canada inadvertently sold fourteen copies of *Half-Blood Prince* early. Those who purchased those books were tracked down and made to sign papers promising not to tell anyone what they read until the book officially went on sale.

By July 15, reports from such faraway places as London, New York, Mexico City, and Sydney, Australia, told of tens of thousands of fans who had lined up in front of bookstores (many had been there for several days) to be the first to get the book at the stroke of midnight.

On July 15, at 11:30 P.M., a car carrying Joanne pulled up in front of Edinburgh Castle. She was surprised that the cover of *Half-Blood Prince* had been projected onto the front of the castle wall. Upon entering the castle she found herself in the middle of a fantasy world. The ancient walls of Edinburgh Castle flickered by the light of countless torches. Roaming the centuries-old rooms and majestic hallways were goblins, clowns, ghosts, fire jugglers, and all manner of mysterious hooded figures.

A roar went up from the hundreds of guests as Joanne was spotted. She waved and happily acknowledged their presence before being ushered into the castle's Great Hall where, as the clock struck midnight, she would read a passage from *Half-Blood Prince* in front of a television camera that would project her words and image to millions.

While she had managed to overcome her shyness of public speaking in the years since the publication of her first book, Joanne was nervous as she entered the Great Hall. She brought forth a copy of *Harry Potter and the Half-Blood Prince* and began to read. But, as she would recall later on her Web site, "It seemed to go alright."

With the cameras turned off, Joanne was now free to relax amid the fantasy and splendor of this coming-out party for the *Half-Blood Prince*. She exchanged pleasantries with the hundreds of children in attendance before meeting with the seventy who had been chosen to interview her. They were each given a signed copy of *Harry Potter and the*

Half-Blood Prince and were instructed to read the book by Sunday so they would have questions to ask her during their press conference.

The three-day celebration continued on Saturday, when Joanne was interviewed by a pair of young Harry Potter fans who had won contests to represent major publications in England and Australia. Hannah Lawson, who represented the *Daily Telegraph*, asked surprisingly in-depth questions regarding the latest book and what the future would hold for Joanne after the last Harry Potter adventure was written.

"I have got to find some meaning after Harry Potter," Joanne said in the *Daily Telegraph*. "I will enjoy spending some time with my children, which I do anyway, but it would be nice to spend maybe a bit more time with them for a while. I know I will keep writing. But what I will write, I don't yet know. I think I will have to get over the shock that Harry is not in my life anymore."

On Sunday, Joanne returned to the castle, where she spent more than an hour answering questions from a full complement of young "cub" reporters. Admittedly, many of the questions asked she had been asked and answered many times before. But coming from so young and enthusiastic a group, her responses were equally enthusiastic and uplifting. As the final day came to a close, Joanne was in a joyous frame of mind.

Within the first twenty-four hours, *Harry Potter and the Half-Blood Prince* had sold out its entire 10.8 million first-edition run. Reports from around the world indicated that copies of the new book were selling at a rate of one every thirteen seconds. Before the weekend was over, *Harry Potter and the Half-Blood Prince* had earned the Guinness World Record Award for being the fastest-selling book in history, having sold more copies in its first twenty-four hours than *The Da Vinci Code* had sold all of the previous year.

Reports began filtering in that Joanne had reportedly made more than a million dollars an hour during the first twenty-four hours of the sale of the new book. Joanne was uncomfortable with those kinds of reports because she knew that there would be more stories and questions focusing on how much money she had made. And sure enough, it was not long before *Forbes* magazine ran an article that claimed that Joanne was the second-richest woman in the world behind Oprah Winfrey. Other stories proclaimed her the richest author in history and estimated her wealth in the billions of dollars.

In an interview with *Dateline NBC,* Joanne joked that, financially, she was doing okay. "These stories are speculating on all possible future earnings and all past earnings. And frankly they're adding figures together that don't exist. I am not a billionaire. I've got plenty of money, more money than I ever dreamed I would have. But I am not a billionaire."

And she was quick to point out in an interview with *Tatler* magazine that while she does maintain three homes in Edinburgh, Perth, and London and does have a moderately sizable staff, she has continued to have rather modest and manageable tastes when it comes to spending her money. "I love a handbag and I love shoes. But I've got a mental limit that I can't spend beyond. I just couldn't."

She acknowledged that she does allow herself a small measure of free spending. A first edition of a Jane Austen book, which cost a pretty penny, sits on her shelf next to some tattered and well-read paperbacks. And she admitted to having once spent an ungodly amount of money on an expensive pair of earrings. But she said that she felt so guilty about that purchase that she immediately wrote out a check for the same amount to a favorite charity.

Her charity work for a variety of causes continued to be uppermost in her heart in the wake of the publication of *Harry Potter and the Half-Blood Prince*. Her two books, *Fantastic Beasts and Where to Find Them* and *Quidditch Through the Ages*, written under the fictional names of Newt Scamander and Kennilworthy Whisp, had raised more than $30 million for Comic Relief, whose goal is to combat worldwide poverty. Another $20 million raised for book sales outside England went to the International Fund for Children and Young People in Crisis. The 1990 death of Joanne's mother from the ravages of multiple sclerosis continued to be a driving force in her charitable good works, with a substantial donation going to the new Centre for Regenerative Medicine at Edinburgh University.

Throughout the remainder of 2005, Joanne continued to work at a fairly leisurely pace. Work on the seventh, yet untitled Harry Potter book was moving slowly and deliberately; giving rise to the fact that Joanne's previous statement that the final Harry Potter book might take two years to complete might, in fact, be a conservative estimate. But the delay was understandable. At just a shade over two years old, David had reached that stage where he was becoming a bit of a handful. And it went without saying that newborn Mackenzie was taking up a lot of Joanne's time.

However, a major consideration in the slow pace of the final Harry Potter book was Joanne's sudden ambivalence about the creation that was about to come to an end. Part of her was anxious that Harry was about to come to an end and that she could get on with the rest of her life, which would, most certainly, find her writing other things. But there was a sadness at the finality of a storyline and characters that had defined her life and made hers a storybook tale all its own.

There were also some internal struggles going on as she worked the storyline into shape. Some new characters were being added. There were storylines to be finally tied up. And, perhaps most important, there was the feeling that some major characters might not live to see the series' final pages.

Including perhaps Harry.

The subject of killing off major characters had

long been a topic of conversation. Beginning with book four, there had been serious talk about eliminating some long-running characters. Joanne's response had always been rather vague, but as the books came and went and certain characters either died or their future was left ambivalent, Joanne more and more had to contend with the question of how the lives and, perhaps, deaths of Harry, Hermione, and Ron might play out in the final chapter.

But when addressing the issue as 2005 neared its end, Joanne remained cryptic on the subject, indicating that she did not want to make any pronouncements until the book was completed so as to avoid being bombarded with hate mail. The reality is that while Joanne had the conclusion of the Harry Potter series in her head long before the first book was published, the fate of her characters has always been up in the air.

Joanne continued to monitor the progress of the film version of *Harry Potter and the Goblet of Fire* and was pleased to hear that director Mike Newell, despite having a background of smaller, independent movies, had been more than capable of handling massive set pieces and powerful special effects while also being able to guide the heart and soul of Joanne's vision to the screen.

Joanne continued a leisurely pace in her life throughout the remainder of 2005. By this time her publishers knew better than to even hint in conversation about when the next book would be completed. They reasoned that, with the final book on the horizon, now was not the time to pester the world's most famous writer for progress reports. After all, *Harry Potter and the Half-Blood Prince* was exceeding all expectations. The book had made its debut atop the world's bestseller lists and the reviews had been excellent.

Much was made this time around of Joanne's ability to continue to breathe new life and a sense of tension and excitement into the book and that Joanne's skills as a writer seemed to be getting better with age. For Joanne, the compliments were outwardly taken with a sense of humility. Inside, she must have been jumping up and down like an excited young girl, because not only had her creation been accepted as a worldwide phenomenon, but her skills as a storyteller of much talent were also being recognized.

Joanne could not be happier.

In November 2005, Joanne journeyed to London for the premiere of *Harry Potter and the Goblet of Fire*. For the author, these annual excursions continued to be a time of laughter and joy. She would meet up with old friends she had not seen since the last premiere, make new acquaintances, and settle in to watch as Hollywood continued to do right by her creation. That *Harry Potter and the Goblet of Fire* would follow the previous films to become a worldwide box office success was almost a given. That it would do so by being true to her vision was a thrill for Joanne that all the money in the world could not buy.

Joanne saw in New Year's 2006 in a fairytale state. She was in the bosom of a loving and supportive family. She was a success in the only occupation she had ever wanted. And for Joanne, the best part was that the dream that had gone on for some sixteen years would continue on for some time.

But the reality was never far from Joanne's mind. Shortly after the new year, she returned to writing the final Harry Potter book.

17

IS HARRY DEAD?

As always seemed to be the case, Joanne's writing could easily be diverted by a call to do good works. In this case, it was a trip to Bucharest, Romania, on January 25 and 26 to help launch the Children's High Level Group, an organization dedicated to helping disabled and mentally handicapped children living in deplorable conditions in psychiatric institutions in eastern European countries like Romania and the Czech Republic.

Joanne's interest in the plight of children virtually living in cages began in 2003, when a newspaper article about these children tugged at her heart. "I almost did not read the article," she recalled in a *Tatler* interview, "but then I thought it was wrong to avoid it. I read the article and I thought 'Why don't I try and do something to help?' "

Joanne began a letter writing campaign directed at the local Scottish members of the European Parliament, the Czech ambassador, Czech prime minister, and Czech president. Through her correspondence, she met with Baroness Emma Nicholson, who had been working on similar issues in Romania. Joanne accepted her invitation to come to Romania on a fact-finding mission. While in Romania, Joanne learned much more about the problems facing the children in these institutions, and she headed up a charity dinner that raised funds for the Children's High Level Group.

Following this trip, Joanne pledged to work with other countries to help bring about change for other institutionalized children of the world. Amid the rush of publicity on the trip to Romania, Joanne was quick to squelch the rumors that she had put aside the writing of the last Harry Potter book indefinitely to do charity work and assured her fans that she was hard at work.

Joanne's worldwide popularity was also beginning to garner the writer a number of rather unusual honors in 2006. An asteroid was named Rowling in her honor. The fossilized remains of a new species of dinosaur was named *Dracorex hogwartsia* in honor of her fictional world. On a much smaller scale, a housing development near her childhood home of Bristol was christened Rowling Gate.

Shortly after Joanne's return from Bucharest, production began on February 6 for the film adaptation of *Harry Potter and the Order of the Phoenix*. The film would be directed by David Yates and, after writing the screenplay for the first four films, Steven Kloves stepped aside in favor of writer Michael Goldenberg. The film was scheduled for a July 13, 2007, release. On the heels of that announcement was the story that pre-production on the film version of *Harry Potter and the Half-Blood Prince* had already begun and, despite the fact that no director or writer had been named to the project, the movie was already slated for a November 21, 2008, unveiling.

Joanne continued to be amazed at the speed that the film industry moved, but she had every confidence, based on the previous films, that Hollywood would continue to get her stories right.

Joanne resumed writing in earnest. And she was finding herself being particularly mum on the topic of this final book. Inquiries as to whether she had even told her husband some of the particulars were met with a laugh during an interview with *Dateline NBC*. "I wouldn't tell Neil. Neil would forget. You know, he wouldn't be a good person to tell anyway. No, no one knows. It's my baby."

Joanne appeared outwardly optimistic about the prospects for the seventh Harry Potter adventure. She acknowledged to her fans on her Web site that she was "really working hard" and that she was "really enjoying it."

But, admittedly, these were trying times for Joanne. Balancing a family with two toddlers running about and attempting to finish what many were openly speculating was the most important work of her career had put Joanne in a distracted state. The level of secrecy had also reached its highest point and was beginning to impact her emotionally.

During one interview in 2006, she nearly blurted out the title of the seventh book before catching herself. Anything remotely connected to the book that was not immediately locked away was now being shredded. And while she tended to shy away from any element of merchandising connected to Harry, she was forced to come out and warn fans that reportedly signed copies of her book that were being auctioned off on Web sites such as eBay were mostly likely forgeries.

As if things could not get any more hectic for Joanne, early in 2006 a notebook containing information on the final Harry Potter book had gone missing. At the time of an interview with the *Tatler,* the notebook had not been found, and it was causing Joanne no small amount of concern.

"I am sure it will turn up." She sighed. "I just hope I didn't leave it somewhere. I have been looking everywhere. What I don't want is for someone to find it and take it to the newspapers."

Given her wealth and celebrity, Joanne was constantly being swamped with requests for financial support, and it took a keen eye and a lot of research to decide which causes to support. In 2006, Joanne found one request particularly interesting. A group of British filmmakers were looking for financing for their short film, entitled *Friday Night Shirt,* which told the story of the struggles of single mothers and featured real single mothers in the title roles. The story and the emphasis on the reality of the life of single mothers struck a powerful chord in Joanne, and she willingly signed on to help get the film made.

Another opportunity to help out worthy charities surfaced in May, when Joanne accepted an offer to fly to America in August to read and answer questions alongside authors Stephen King and John Irving in New York City's Radio City Hall. The two-day event would support the Haven Foundation (an organization dedicated to helping out performing artists who, through accidents and illness, are unable to work) and Doctors Without Borders (a group that delivers emergency medical aid around the world), and would allow Joanne the first opportunity to read in America since 2000.

Joanne was making few public appearances at this point, preferring to spend her time with her family and in writing. But during an appearance on the *Richard and Judy* television show, she set tongues to wagging when she openly talked about the possibility of favorite Harry Potter characters dying in the final book.

"One character got a reprieve," she said during

the interview. "But I have to say that two die that I didn't intend to die."

Joanne told the hosts that she refused to elaborate on which characters were being killed off because she did not want to start receiving hate mail from irate fans. Joanne would not say if one of the characters who would die was Harry. But she stirred the pot the next minute when she said, "I've never been tempted to kill him off before the final book because I've always planned on seven books and I want to finish on seven books."

Joanne knew she had opened a Pandora's box as soon as she said the words, but it was too late to take it all back. Almost immediately the worldwide press jumped on her remarks and, by such diverse outlets as the fan-based Leaky Cauldron Web site, *BBC News* and *CBS News,* broadcast her comments around the world. And, as often happens, many of these outlets slanted the story to indicate that Joanne was most certainly going to kill off Harry Potter in the final book.

Joanne barely had time to contemplate the impact her words were having, for on June 25, she journeyed from her home in Edinburgh at the re-

quest of Queen Elizabeth to be a part of the celebration of the queen's eightieth birthday being
held at Buckingham Palace. Joanne would read
aloud a section of *Harry Potter and the Half-Blood
Prince* for the queen and a reported two thousand
children who had been invited to the event. The
proceedings also included an elaborate show in
which an owl was released from the palace and sent
on its way to Hogwarts, where, in a prerecorded
segment filmed on the set of the film *Harry Potter
and the Order of the Phoenix,* Harry, Ron, and
Neville receive the owl and end up saving the storyline's fictional crisis with a bit of Muggles magic.

Joanne was thrilled with the splendor of the day
and related in BC Books' coverage of the event
how she thought "This was a most wonderful way
to celebrate the queen's eightieth birthday."

Try as she might, Joanne could not escape the
expected press coverage of the event and the inevitable questions about how book seven was coming. "I am feeling sad that it is the last one. But so
far so good. I'm doing well, I think. You can never
really tell until you get near the end. I am not quite
there yet."

When the possible death of Harry Potter had run its course in the press, the questions most often put to Joanne were about her writing life post-Harry. She had hinted in recent years that there were bits and pieces of other kinds of writing sitting inside her desk but would not share the particulars of what they were. One thing she did indicate in a CBBC news conference was that there was little chance of another long fantasy series in her future.

"I don't think I will write any more fantasy books," she said. "The reason for that is that I have now written a huge, long fantasy. I think I have put my best ideas into Harry Potter and if I were to try and write another fantasy, I would feel it was second best. I would like Harry to be my one and only stab at the genre."

While excited at the prospect of flying to New York in August, Joanne had no intention of putting aside her writing during the trip. And so the manuscript of the final Harry Potter adventure, much of it in handwritten form, was carefully packed in her baggage. During the long flight, Joanne would take out the manuscript and could be seen scribbling words onto paper as the plane winged its way across the Atlantic. Many of those on board quickly recognized Joanne but, out of respect for her privacy, left her alone.

There was a sense of excitement in Joanne as she looked out the plane window as it circled the New York airport. Although she would miss her family terribly, even for just this couple of days, there was also the thrill of being abroad in another land, meeting her fans, and being around authors she respected. For Joanne, this was a fantasy come true.

Her initial meeting with authors Stephen King and John Irving began things on a positive note. They were polite, cordial, respectful of her work, and possessed a different kind of humor than she was used to at home. All three got along famously.

During a press conference held before the event, King and Irving, caught up in all the fervor of who would die in the final book, pleaded with Joanne not to kill off Harry. Rowling responded by saying that she would make no promises.

At that same press conference, reporters once again questioned Joanne about how she felt about the series coming to an end. Her response, posted in various articles and Web sites, including the Harry Potter Automatic News Aggregator, acknowledged that her emotions at this point were mixed.

"On the one hand, I'm going to feel sad. Harry's been an enormous part of my life. It's been a turbulent phase in my life and he was always the constant. So there will be a sense of bereavement. There are pressures in writing something as popular as Harry. Wonderful though it's been, I think that there will also be a certain freedom in escaping that particular part of writing Harry Potter."

Advance word on the two-day event had been good. The idea of seeing and hearing any of the three was a powerful attraction. But combining three authors of their calibre into one event was something that the public just had to witness, and so both shows sold out in short order.

Even at this point in her career, Joanne still felt the butterflies before she was to speak before large groups, and the New York appearances were no exception. But once she and the other authors were introduced to thunderous applause, the nerves immediately disappeared.

Joanne's introduction by actress Kathy Bates set the stage for a spirited reading of *Harry Potter and the Half-Blood Prince* and a probing question-and-

answer session that followed. One of the questions
centered on whether or not the character of Dumbledore was definitely dead. Joanne said yes.

"Dumbledore is definitely dead," she disclosed
at the session. "I know that there are a lot of people
out there who are not going to like that answer."

At one point in the questioning of the authors,
Stephen King admitted to the audience that there
were passages in Joanne's books, especially when it
came to the characters of the Death Eaters, that really frightened him. Joanne was heard to quip,
"Imagine having scared Stephen King."

Although it would not come to light until later,
Joanne had a breakthrough of sorts regarding the
seventh book. To that point, she had been juggling
several possible titles for the final book. But while
showering on her second day in New York, she had
a revelation and a title.

Joanne encountered a bit of a problem as she
readied to board the plane that would take her
back to England after the New York visit. She had
had no problem carrying her bulky manuscript
aboard the plane going to America, but on the return flight she was momentarily blocked by security who felt her manuscript was a suspicious

package that threatened security. After a few moments a compromise was reached and Joanne was allowed to bring her manuscript aboard the plane as long as it was bound up in rubber bands.

"Thankfully they let me take it on," she reported on her Web site. "I don't know what I would have done if they hadn't; sailed home probably."

Joanne would continue to be forthcoming with her fans as she continued to work on book seven. Regular updates on her Web site indicated that she was hard at work and was dealing with the reality of writing scenes that had been planned out more than a dozen years earlier. She admitted in the same Web site entry that she was now both overwhelmed and elated at the writing of the last Harry Potter book.

"I don't think anyone can possibly know how this feels," she told her fans. "I both want and don't want to finish this book."

She also acknowledged that, as with the previous book, she was once again out and about, writing sections of the book at an undisclosed café and, apparently, drawing little interest from passersby who had come to recognize Joanne at work as just another tourist attraction in Edinburgh.

By now, Joanne was so caught up in all things Harry that, for the first time, she was having dreams about Harry in his world in which she actually saw herself as Harry wandering through her world in a surreal adventure. When disclosing this to her fans on her Web site, she laughingly said, "Perhaps I should cut back on the caffeine."

To relax from the pressures of writing, Joanne was now making sporadic visits to the set of *Harry Potter and the Order of the Phoenix,* where she watched scenes being filmed and chatted with the actors. She continued to marvel at the expansive sets and locations and how modern movie-making technology was once again bringing her fantasies to life.

As usual, there continued to be rumors to deal with and dispel. One was that the final book was going to be in excess of 750 pages in length. She categorically denied that and denied the recurring story that, way back when, she was the one responsible for Steven Spielberg not getting the directing job on the first Harry Potter film.

Joanne had finally come to a decision on the final book's title and, on December 21, 2006, announced it as *Harry Potter and the Deathly*

Hallows. What many did not realize was that by the time that announcement was made, Joanne had all but completed the manuscript and was in the process of putting the finishing touches on Harry's last adventure.

Joanne was mentally exhausted. There was a sense of both relief and sadness at finally putting Harry Potter to rest. There was also the romantic in her that wanted to do something special to commemorate the end of an important time in her life.

Shortly after the first of the year, Joanne snuck into room 652 of the Balmoral Hotel in Edinburgh to add one final flourish to the Harry Potter odyssey.

18

THE END . . .

Joanne stared down at the mountain of manuscript pages in front of her. She made a final series of notations on the page in front of her and then put down her pen. The calendar said January 11, 2007.

The date would be remembered as the day Joanne wrote the final words in the odyssey of Harry Potter.

Joanne sat quietly, contemplating the true end to this stage of her life and career. Always more humble than ego-driven, she suddenly felt a need to, somehow, document this moment in literary history. She looked around the room. Her eyes fell on a decorative marble bust of the god Hermes. She picked up a marking pen, went to the bust, and started to write:

"J. K. Rowling finished writing *Harry Potter and the Deathly Hallows* in this room (652) on 11th Jan 2007."

She then signed the bust with a flourish.

Word quickly leaked to the worldwide press that the last book in the Harry Potter series was done. Once the initial excitement over the announcement began to subside, reporters got wind of the story of the signed bust and swarmed the Balmoral Hotel to get the rest of the story.

The general manager of the hotel, Debbie Taylor, would only confirm, in a story in *The Scotsman,* that Joanne had, indeed, signed a bust following a recent visit to the hotel and that, presently, the bust was being kept in safekeeping by the hotel. She further stated that the hotel had no plans on turning the room into a tourist shrine.

Hotel spokesperson Jessica Trotter told *CNN.com* that "Obviously this is quite a unique case. We're honored and flattered she chose the Balmoral as surroundings to do her writing."

The story would be a short-lived curiosity that quickly gave way to the renewed excitement over the completion of the last book in the Harry Potter series. In early February, it was announced that *Harry Potter and the Deathly Hallows* would officially go on sale July 21, 2007. Shortly thereafter, Warner Bros. announced that the film *Harry Potter and the Order of the Phoenix* would be released July 13, 2007.

Fans around the world were thrilled that much of their summer plans would revolve around the world of Harry Potter. The excitement was inevitably followed by a sense of sadness that the door to the adventures of Harry Potter would soon be closing forever.

With the last book behind her, Joanne was now attempting to settle back into a normal routine. There was still the expected editing of the manuscript to contend with, but, for the most part, her days were spent enjoying the normal family routines that she so enjoyed and, in reflective moments, dealing with her emotions in regards to Harry. And as she would readily admit in entries on her Web site that would also appear on the Leaky Cauldron fan Web site and in an article in *The Scotsman,* her emotions were all over the place.

"I always knew that Harry's story would end with the seventh book," she said, "but saying good-bye has been just as hard as I always knew it would be. Even while I'm mourning, though, I feel an incredible sense of achievement. I can hardly believe that I've finally written the ending I've been planning for so many years. I've never felt such an extreme mixture of moments in my life. I never dreamed that I could feel, simultaneously, heartbroken, and euphoric."

She also expressed her feelings on the recently completed *Deathly Hallows.* Joanne said that the book was "my favorite" and that it was "the most wonderful way to end the series."

Shortly after the announcement of the release date for *Deathly Hallows,* bookstores began taking early orders for the book. The results were amazing. Early orders were more than, 500 percent higher than they had been for *Half-Blood Prince.* Months in advance of its actual release, *Deathly Hallows* had skyrocketed to number one on several bookstore Web sites, most notably *Amazon.com* and *Barnes&Noble.com*. Joanne, who normally left the business side of her creative endeavors to others, was shocked upon hearing the news.

Before she went back to the important business of being a wife and mother, Joanne received good news on a non-Harry-related matter when she was informed that the short film she had financed, *Friday Night Shirt,* had captured an award for the best dramatic short film at the High Definition International Film Festival.

With little in the way of actual news now forthcoming, the rumor mill was once again working overtime. Most of it was centering on the reported death of at least two characters in the final book. Joanne would goodnaturedly deny the more outrageous stories, but at one time laughingly stirred the pot by saying that she may well have killed off everybody in the final book. Fearing that people might take even this obvious quip seriously, she instantly said she was only joking.

One of the more outrageous and yet somewhat believable stories hit the media—that Joanne had signed a letter of intent with the Disney Company that would allow the theme park kings to begin development on an attraction involving the Harry

Potter characters. In short order, legal representatives for Joanne came forward to say that there was no such letter of intent between Joanne and Disney.

Still other rumors persisted that Joanne had burned herself out writing the Harry Potter books and would never write another word. At the other end of the spectrum were notions that Joanne would turn her attention to writing adult mysteries and that some of her future work might be written under a pseudonym. At the extreme end of the rumor landscape was the emerging idea that Joanne Kathleen Rowling had been a pseudonym all along and that she would now begin writing under her real name.

Joanne patiently attempted to address the stories. Yes, her name was really Joanne Kathleen Rowling. No, she had never thought of writing under another name post–Harry Potter. But she did concede that, over the years, she had written other things besides Harry Potter.

"I have written other things that have not been published, which I assure you is no great loss to the world," she told interviewers at the Edinburgh Book Festival. "I have written all sorts of different things but nothing that has been published. Some of it might be published one day. There are some unfinished things that I would quite like to finish, but I do not know that I would want them to be published."

But with the end of Harry Potter near, she said that there would be a writing life after Harry. She revealed late in 2006 that she had recently completed several short stories and that she had completed another, as yet untitled, children's book, which she describes as "a political fairy story" about a monster that would appeal to young readers. Joanne also speculated that, while she would not write an eighth Harry Potter book, she might publish an encyclopedia of the Harry Potter world, consisting of unpublished material and notes, whose proceeds would be given to charity.

Joanne did admit to a certain amount of insecurity regarding any future writing efforts at the Edinburgh Book Festival. "We'll have to see if any of it is good enough to be published. I mean, obviously that is a great concern because the first thing I write post-Harry could be absolutely dreadful and people will buy it. So you're left with this real insecurity."

With the editing done, Joanne was without

some kind of deadline for the first time in nearly ten years. It amused her that she could suddenly do absolutely anything. She traveled, did charity work, and just played at being a mom. Joanne was passing through the stage in which she was terrified at the prospect of nothing to do.

"Now I find it liberating," she said in a *Dateline NBC* interview. "The world is my oyster. I can do whatever I like."

Well, not quite.

As the weeks ticked down to both the publication of *Harry Potter and the Deathly Hallows* and the release of the film version of *Harry Potter and the Order of the Phoenix,* Joanne found herself obligated to do a certain amount of press. Rather than feeling pressure, Joanne fielded the numerous interviews with ease. Of the movie, she was uniformally positive in recalling her visits to the set and how well Hollywood had thus far treated her creation. A lot of the questions regarding the book were pretty much the same questions she had been hearing for more than a year, and so it was easy to toss off variations on her standard responses. Joanne was steadfast on not spilling the secret of who dies in the final book, and she succeeded in fueling the sense of mystery that would have millions of readers racing to bookstores to find out the answer to the final mystery.

The celebration of the arrival of *Harry Potter and the Deathly Hallows* had, like previous books, taken on a circus atmosphere. Bookstores around the world were planning fantasy-themed events tied into the new book. Web sites had installed clocks that were constantly counting down the months, weeks, days, hours, and seconds to the release of the book. Signs were everywhere.

The press was working overtime to discuss Harry Potter in every possible way. *Entertainment Weekly* took the approach in a 2007 article that Joanne's publisher and countless bookstores would see a decline in fortune without new Harry Potter adventures on a regular basis and ended with a snide speculation on how Joanne might be persuaded to come out of retirement to write another Harry Potter book once her financial status had shrunk from billions to millions. Joanne reportedly had a good laugh at the notion that anything could persuade her to write another Harry Potter book.

It was reported in the newspaper *Cape Argus* that one bookstore was readying what they called a "distress area" for the day the book went on sale to comfort those who would become emotionally upset when they discovered which characters in the book died.

The subject of characters dying in the final book had become such a controversy that the *Citizen* newspaper reported that the University of New Hampshire British literature expert James Krasner had his own predictions on who would live and die.

"There is no way Harry will die," he said. "Harry won't die because these are comic stories in which good has to win."

Krasner went on to state that "Lord Voldemort has to die. And Snape, who is really fighting for good despite all appearances, will likely die. Neville Longbottom is really the chosen one, so I suspect he will die."

By the time July rolled around, Harry Potter mania was in full swing. Web sites such as the Leaky Cauldron and Mugglenet were reporting the slightest bit of news regarding the upcoming movie and the last book. Sites were abuzz with opinions on the movie and alleged reports from people who claimed to have already seen *Order of the Phoenix.*

As Joanne prepared to see the movie with a live audience for the first time, she was awash in emotion. She could be sure that the film would enhance the fantasy world she had created in the minds of millions of young readers. And she felt that the remaining films in the odyssey would fill a void left by the end of the Harry Potter experience.

The final book was a whole other matter. Try as she might, it was difficult for Joanne to come to grips with the idea that she would never write about Harry and his world again. She was anxious to move onto other things and excited about continuing to challenge herself as a writer. But in a sense she was already seeing the ghosts of Harry, Ron, and Hermione peeking out from corners, saying good-bye, and she was having a hard time doing the same.

Those closest to Joanne, her husband and their children as well as her sister and close family and friends, were quite aware of what Joanne was going through. They were thoughtful listeners when Joanne came to them with her feelings and concerns. They offered their opinions only when asked. But at the end of the day, they knew any decisions would ultimately be made by her.

Word was already beginning to surface about the movie version of *Harry Potter and the Half-Blood Prince,* which was scheduled to start filming early in 2008. Veteran production designer Stuart Craig had already signed on and was tantalizing reporters with what wonders would be created for that film. It was also announced that, because new British locations had become harder to find, a good portion of the movie might be filmed in parts of Ireland. However, keeping up with news on the movie proved only a temporary escape from the real task at hand for Joanne, which was accompanying Harry on his final adventure.

It would be as if the world had come to a sudden halt on July 20—Television, radio, and newspapers full of stories about the release of *Harry Potter and the Deathly Hallows.* So-called experts brought in to explain what it all meant. Boxes of books under the tightest of security.

Stores around the world preparing to stay open all night, planning Harry parties and all manner of activities surrounding the release of the book. Cities large and small alive with children walking the streets in costumes depicting their favorite characters. Lines forming outside bookstores; children chattering excitedly about what new secrets the final book would reveal.

At the stroke of midnight, screams of joy would echo around the world as *Harry Potter and the Deathly Hallows* was unveiled to the world. Children held their copies tightly. Many found corners of the bookstore where they had made their purchase and immediately began reading. Within minutes shrieks of excitement would be heard as the mysteries of this final adventure began to be revealed.

On July 21, 2007, lights all over the world would blink well into the night as millions of young readers filled their heads with the wonder of it all.

19

. . . AND THE
BEGINNING

Inevitably Joanne would spend the next weeks giving selected readings, interviews, and dealing with all kinds of questions in the wake of the release of *Harry Potter and the Deathly Hallows*. And then there would be the reaction of her young readers.

Many would be surprised and shocked at the revelations of the final book. There would be questions galore as to why Joanne had chosen to kill off the characters she did. There would also be universal praise for the way in which she wrapped up the seven-year odyssey and sent the characters of Hogwarts out into the world. In conversations after the release of the book, Joanne once again would be both patient and direct in addressing the particulars of *Deathly Hallows* and of her own future.

"I don't think I'm ever going to have anything like Harry again," she had stated in an interview on the *Richard and Judy Show*. "You just get one like Harry."

Joanne's heart was on her sleeve when she talked to *Dateline NBC*. "It's going to be really emotional to say good-bye. I'm going to find it very difficult. But it must be done. It's been a fabulous ride but you have to know when to get off and I know when to get off."

Joanne would be heartened by the worldwide reception her book received. Surely, the nearly 11 million first-edition copies would sell out in a matter of days, immediately catapulting *Harry Potter and the Deathly Hallows* to the top of several important bestseller lists and eclipsing the uproar of the release of the recent movie. Many would proclaim July 2007 as the month of Harry Potter. But it very easily could have been called the year of

Harry Potter for, as July turned into August and beyond, Harry Potter would be everywhere. The inevitable toys and other forms of commercial merchandizing would flood the market, but Joanne would be heartened by the fact that the real interest continued to be in the books and the movies.

Following her promotional duties, Joanne would assume a lower profile. She would spend the next months reportedly being the dutiful mother and wife. The family would do some traveling and entertain their close circle of family and friends. For the first time in nearly a decade, Joanne would be able to truly unwind and relax.

However, the press would not completely let go. Once the uproar over the final book died down, newspaper and Internet speculation and rumor would continue regarding Joanne's future. Some speculating that Joanne had been a writer with one very good idea who would never write again. Others putting forth the notion that Joanne would take a year or two off before attempting another book. The more hopeful offering that Joanne had already struck a multimillion-dollar deal with her publishers to write an eighth Harry

Potter book that would be out in 2008 to coincide with the release of the movie version of *Harry Potter and the Half-Blood Prince.*

Joanne would be quick to dismiss any and all speculation as rubbish, or she just would not comment, which only succeeds in fueling the speculation of what might be coming next.

One thing is certain. Joanne Kathleen Rowling had secured her place in literary history. The Harry Potter books would continue on through the ages as a flight of fantasy that would beguile readers old and young to pick up on what many perceived as the dying art of reading. The movies would prove timeless classics. And she had long ago acknowledged that even though the books would eventually stop, the questions would continue to come. Which is why she has stated she will never shut down her official Web site.

"My feeling is I couldn't possibly answer all the questions because the novel is the wrong form for which, for example, to present a catalogue of a character's favorite colors," she said in a 2005 joint interview with reporters from The Leaky Cauldron and Mugglenet. "So, I'm never going to be able to answer everything that an obsessive fan would want to know in the novels. Also, I think people will continue to theorize about characters even after book seven."

In that same interview, Joanne, perhaps seeing the future, talked about how Neil and she continued to lead their children through a fairly normal life and would continue to present a grounded picture for them when it was all over and done.

"Keeping our kids grounded, normal, and rooted in the real world has always been my top priority in life. Things like living in a castle and such have had very little effect on them. I think as much as we can, we do lead a pretty normal life. We go out to the shops and walk around town like everyone else. All three children will grow up seeing Neil and I working. There are no plans on either of our parts to stop working, put our feet up, and go yachting around the world. We'll keep working, and I think that's a pretty good example to set for your children. Self-worth really lies in finding out what you do best."

Perhaps toward the end of 2007, reports will begin to surface of Joanne once again being spotted at tables at out-of-the-way Edinburgh coffee shops, jotting down sentences and notes on sheets of paper.

The stories may also begin to spread that on some nights, after putting David and Mackenzie to bed, Joanne would go off the farthest reaches of the castle, go into her office, and would not come out into well into the early morning hours.

Was it another Harry Potter? Something completely different? Or was it simply all a fantasy conjured up by the legions of fans who after a decade of fantasy that had sparked their imaginations and defined their lives . . .

Were hoping for something more.